NEXT LEVEL
DEEP MACHINE LEARNING

Complete Tips and Tricks to Deep Machine Learning

Joe Grant

Table of Contents

Introduction

The scientific study of statistical data and algorithms used by computers to perform assigned tasks without having any explicit instructions is known as Machine Learning. In this method, computers rely on inference and patterns. It is a branch of artificial intelligence. A mathematical model builds on sample data, known as training data, and is used by machine learning algorithms to make decisions and predictions regarding the assigned task. There is a wide variety of applications where machine learning algorithms can be used, such as computer vision, email filtering, online customers support, spam filtering, product recommendations, social media services, and to perform other tasks where it is impossible or difficult to develop a conventional algorithm.

Deep learning is a branch of machine learning. To understand the concept of deep learning, one has to understand the concept and basics of machine learning completely. Machine learning is comprised of learning algorithms that are used by the computers in performing a task without having any explicit instructions. Learning algorithms can be explained through an example of a linear regression algorithm. After that, we will move towards the concept of how computers fit existing data and find patterns that convert it into new generalize data. Most machine learning algorithms are based on settings called hyperparameters, which are adjusted separately by using additional data. Hyperparameters must be determined external and separate from learning algorithms. Machine learning interprets and processes data on the basis of statistics. The only difference between machine learning and the conventional way of using statistical data is that, in machine learning, there is increased emphasis on computers to statistically solve complicated functions and decreased emphasis on manual usage of formulas to interpret statistical data. Two major statistic approaches are Frequentist estimators and Bayesian inference.

Machine Learning algorithms can be further categorized into Supervised Learning and Unsupervised Learning. These categories of machine learning will be explained with examples further in this chapter. Deep Learning algorithms process data on the basis of an optimization algorithm called stochastic gradient descent. We will explain to you how to build a machine learning algorithm by combining various algorithm components such as a cost function, a model, an optimization algorithm, and a dataset. In the later section, you will also get an understanding of the factors that limits the ability of traditional machine learning to generalize. These limiting factors are motivational drivers that played an important role in the development of deep learning algorithms that can overcome these obstacles.

Defining Learning Algorithms

A machine learning algorithm is a type of algorithm that is capable of learning from data. According to Mitchell (1997), the definition of machine learning in this regard means, "A computer program is said to learn from experience "E" in a tasks "T" and performance measure "P", if its performance in a particular task in "T", as measured by "P", improves with experience "E". There can be variety of experiences "E", tasks "T" and measure performance "P". You will not find a formal definition of these entities in this book. Instead of this, we will provide you with some descriptions and examples of different kinds of task, performance measures, and experiences which will help you with developing a machine learning algorithm.

The Task, "T"

Sometimes programs are written and designed by human begins are not able to solve complicated tasks, and at this point, machine learning takes the lead and solves all the difficult tasks in no time. This point completely justifies the importance of machine learning. Developing an understanding of machine learning will help you in understanding the principles that underlie artificial intelligence.

Defining the word "Task" in the process of machine learning can be tricky. The process of learning itself is not a task. The ability to perform the task requires learning. In this sense, learning is the means of attaining the ability to perform the task. For example, if you design a robot and want it to walk than walking is the task assigned to a robot. You can program the robot to learn how to walk, or you can run a program directly manually that can guide the robot about how to walk.

The machine-learning task can be defined as the process by which the machine adapts and solves a problem. This is basically the sum of the measurements of an object or a particular event. The person ideally wants the machine to adapt to the process. Vector is used to represent the example, and other entries are also identified by different vectors. As you know that the pixel values are used to identify different features of the images, and the machines use different values to identify the parts of the image. Some tasks that are performed by the machines are listed below:

Classification: The machine classifies the parameters into different categories. Different functions are produced to categorize the parameters. The input function is defined by vector X. Some other variants are also used when the machine is classifying the objects. Some other variants in the classification parameter are f variant and k variant. When you input an image for classification, the output code is received that is used to specify the things in the image. Face recognition through computers uses this concept of object recognition, and you can witness this technology when tagging people in different photo collections, and their names will automatically display on their faces.

Classification with Missing Inputs: When the computer programs are not guaranteed to receive every measurement in its input vector, then classification becomes more challenging and difficult. The classification task can only be solved when the learning algorithm has to define a single function with a complete set of data from vector inputs to a categorical output. In case when inputs are missing, the learning algorithm must learn a set of functions to provide an output, rather than just providing a single input function. Such situations frequently arise in medical diagnosis when most tests are expensive or can be harmful to the patient. This problem can be effectively solved by applying a probability distribution over all relevant variables than solve the classification task by marginalizing the missing variables of input. By putting n input variables, you can get 2^n different functions that can be used in each possible set of missing inputs. Even for the joint probability distribution, you only need to learn a single classification function.

Regression: The task in which the computer program is asked to predict a numerical value to the given input is known as regression. This task is solved by the learning algorithm with the help of an output function f: Rn $\rightarrow$ R. Regression task is similar to classification task but only differs in the format of the output. Regression task can be explained through an example of an insurance claim. In this task, the computer program is to make a prediction of the expected claim amount that an insured person will make regarding insurance premium or the prediction of anticipated future price of securities. These predictions are also very beneficial in algorithm trading.

Transcription: The task in which the computer learning system is assigned to observe the unstructured representation of data and convert it into discrete, textual form is known as Transcription. For example, in optical character recognition, a photograph containing an image of text is shown to the computer program and is asked to convert this text in the form of a sequence of characters. The method of deep learning can also be seen in the Google Street view, which processes address and street numbers. Speech recognition is another example in which an audio wave file is provided to the computer program, which converts the sequence of characters or word ID codes describing the words that were recorded in the audio through speaking. In modern speech recognition systems, deep learning is a crucial component that is used by major companies such as Google, Microsoft, and IBM.

Machine Translation: In this type of task, input given to the computer program is already in the form of symbols or in any machine language, and the computer program is asked to convert the given input into another language by using the sequence of symbols. This task is normally applied to natural human speaking languages, such as the conversion of the English language into the French language. Recently, Deep learning is becoming popular in performing such tasks.

Structured Output: Structured output can be explained as a task in which the output is a vector (multiple values in a data structure) having a close relationship between different elements. An example of a structured task can be parsing – means dividing a sentence of natural language into a tree of grammatical structure and related nodes of trees as being nouns, verbs, or adverbs, and so on. Pixel-wise segmentation of images is another example of a structured task where the computer program assigns a specific category to every pixel of an image. In this regard, an example of deep learning is to annotate the locations of roads using aerial photographs. The output doesn't have to be exact as input, but it should be as close as in these annotation-style tasks. An example of this is image captioning in which the computer program processes an image and describe the image in a natural language sentence as an output. These tasks are known as structured output tasks because the program gives several output values which are tightly interlinked with each other. For example, the words describing an image as output must form an understandable sentence.

Anomaly Detection: Anomaly detection is a task in which the computer program runs through a series of events or objects and points out some of them as being inappropriate and unusual. Anomaly detection can be used in credit card fraud detection. Through observing your credit card purchasing habits, Credit Card Company can detect and prevent misuse of your cards. In case your credit card information or your credit card gets stolen, the thief will use your card in a different manner than your purchasing habit. This will not only inform the credit card company but will also help the owner in blocking the credit card service to avoid its misuse. In order to prevent fraud, some credit card companies also hold payment of uncharacteristic purchases, which are against the purchasing habit of the credit card owner.

Synthesis and Sampling: The task in which the computer program is commanded to generate new examples that are relevant to those which are given in the sample data. Application of synthesis and sampling task can be seen in media applications where it can be boring and expensive for an artist to create a large volume of unique content on his own. For example, video games are capable of automatically creating textures for landscapes and objects rather than requiring an artist to perform the task manually. There are cases when synthesis or sampling procedures are required to create specific output from the given input data. This can be explained through an example of a speech synthesis task. In this task, a written sentence is provided to the computer program and asked to convert it into an audio waveform containing a spoken version of the given sentence. This is a type of structured output task with some added qualification. Each input doesn't have a single correct output, and a large amount of variation in the output can be seen to look natural and realistic.

Denoising: This is a task in which the computer program is given an input of a corrupted example, which is found in a clean example. The corruption is due to unknown error in the file. The machine uses different algorithms to find the right sections and the corrupted version of the program. If it could not find the corrupted version, it would predict the p-value, also known as a conditional probability distribution.

Probability Mass Function Estimation or Density Estimation: The computer will use the algorithm to find the probability density function. To complete this task, the machine learns the entire architecture of the file that is provided to it. The machine will find the example cluster in the file and examine it. Distribution is known by finding the density estimation of the file. When the distribution is calculated, all the other tasks are performed easily.

The Performance Measure, "P"

Good architecture is formulated to calculate the performance of the machine. The speed of machine learning depends on how fast the machine can solve the problems and what is the success ratio of the machine. When a system performs a specific task, the performance measure is completed by the system.

If you have some values of the inputs missing, then we use the accuracy of the model to find out its efficiency. Accuracy can be defined as the correct output ratio of the machine. By this, you can also find the error rate of the machine that is proportionate to the accuracy of the model. The higher the accuracy, the lower will be the error rate and vice versa. The error rate is usually referred to as 0-1 loss. These calculations are very important when you measure the performance of the machine and its capability to learn and solve new problems. Not all tasks in the machine learning revolve around the error rate or accuracy. When you need to evaluate the density estimation, the 0-1 loss and error rate becomes irrelevant, and you need to use another performance metric to find the score of the example. Average log-reporting is a viable way to find the density estimation of the example.

Test data is used to find these values as we would want to see the performance of the machine in a real-world environment. The training data is ignored when we are working on these performance metrics, as finding the performance in a real-world scenario is our main priority. The choice of the performance metric is objective, and it does not provide the information related to the read performance of the machine. Different factors need to be applied when you are looking to find the read performance of the machine. The user should understand the type of machine and its application, and this will help him to decide which tasks need to be measured.

In rare cases, it is very difficult to find and measure the metrics of the machine. For example, the density estimation and the probability distribution of the model are implicit at times, and this is when you need to design a new criterion that evaluates the objective of the example.

The Experience, "E"

There are two basic types of machine learning algorithms. They are known as supervised and unsupervised algorithms. In this section, we will provide the basic information about these algorithms and how you can differentiate them. Most algorithms in this book use the entire dataset, and you need to understand the basic concept of the dataset and their types to understand the working of algorithms. Different examples sum up into a dataset or collection of data analyzed by the machine. You can also refer to the datasets as data points. The algorithms perform the basic and advanced functions in the machine. Here is the example of two learning algorithms in deep machine learning.

Supervised Learning Algorithms

As far as the supervised learning algorithms in machine learning are concerned, they study the features of the example, and all the features are represented with a target or label. Take the iris dataset; for example, the supervised learning algorithm will study and classify the iris plans and differentiate them into three species. The algorithm will study the measurements of the plants to differentiate them.

Unsupervised Learning Algorithms

The unsupervised learning algorithm studies the entire dataset and identify, and study the useful properties of the example or dataset. With the help of unsupervised learning algorithms, we can study the entire probability distribution of an example. Tasks like denoising and synthesis can be performed adequately with the help of unsupervised learning algorithms.

You can find the value of x in the probability distribution of machine learning with the help of these algorithms. Here the target y acts as a teacher or an instructor that guides the machine learning system what to do. The term supervised learning is based on this concept. On the other hand, there is no teacher or instructor in unsupervised learning; the algorithm must learn how to make sense of the date without having any guide.

Both terms unsupervised learning and supervised are not formally defined. It is normally hard to differentiate the lines between both. Many machine learning programs are capable of performing both tasks.

Linear Regression

The machine learning algorithm is defined as an algorithm used to improve the performance of a computer's program at some tasks with the help of experience obtained from other tasks. For more understanding, it can be explained through a simple example of a machine learning algorithm known as linear regression. According to the name, all kind of regression problems is solved with the help of linear regression. The purpose is to design a system that is capable of taking a vector x ∈ Rn as input and predict its output as the value of a scalar y ∈ R. In linear regression cases; a linear function is the output of all inputs. Let ˆy is the value that y should take on in the model. Output can be defined as y = wTx, where w ∈ Rn is a vector of parameters.

To control the behavior of the system, certain values are used known as Parameters.

Capacity, Overfitting, and Underfitting

The main challenge of the machine learning algorithm is that we perform new unseen inputs rather than using the same input, which is used in the training mode of the model. The capability to perform well on unseen inputs is called generalization.

A training set is used as a learning model to train the machine learning algorithm. In the training set, we can compute some error measures called the training error, which can be used to reduce the training error. According to the discussion, it is simply an optimization problem. To separate optimization from machine learning, "generalization error," also known as "test error," is to be low. Expect the value of error on the new input is known as generalization error. The expectation of error is applied to different possible inputs taken from the probability distribution of inputs. It is expected that the system will witness such inputs in practice.

In the data generating process, data is mostly generated through the probability distribution over datasets. Use the collective set of assumptions known as i.i.d. Assumptions are examples in each dataset and are independent of each other. It will describe the data generating process with a probability distribution over a single example.

Underfitting and Overfitting are the two challenging factors in the machine learning algorithm. Underfitting is a condition when the model is unable to detect a significantly low error value on the training set. Overfitting is the situation when the gap between the test error and training error is large enough to cover.

The problem of underfitting and overfitting of the model can be controlled by altering its capacity. A model capacity is the ability of the model to fit a large variety of functions. In low capacity models, the only training set can be adjusted. High capacity models are capable of overfitting as they have the memorizing properties of the training set.

Learning algorithm capacity can be controlled by choosing its hypothesis space, the set of functions used by learning algorithms to provide solutions. For example, a set of all linear functions are used as inputs as its hypothesis in the linear regression algorithm. In hypothesis space, polynomials can be used in the linear regression rather than just a linear function to generalize. This will increase the model's capacity.

To get the best result from the machine learning algorithm, it is important to set their capacity according to the complexity of the task and the amount of training data they need to perform well. Insufficient capacity of models is not able to solve complex tasks.

Models with high capacity are capable of solving complex tasks, and in the case when the capacity is higher than required to solve the given task, they may overfit.

Till now, we have only discussed one method of changing the capacity of the model that is through changing the number of input features and simultaneously adding new parameters linked to those features. There are also many other ways to change the capacity of the model. The choice of a model doesn't only determine the capacity. In order to reduce a training objective, the model specifics which functions the learning algorithm can choose when differentiating the parameters. This process is called the representational capacity of the model. In many cases, the optimization problem may occur when the learning algorithm tries to find the best function. In reality, the learning algorithm doesn't find the best function but only chooses that function, which reduces the training error. Limitation such as problem in the optimization algorithm indicates learning algorithm's effective capacity may be less than the representational capacity of the model.

Modern ways to improve the generalization of machine learning models to purify the thought process from the inception or as early as possible. The principle of parsimony was introduced by early scholars who are widely known as Occam's razor.

The statistical learning hypothesis gives different methods for evaluating the model limit. Among these, the most outstanding is the Vapnik-Chervonenkis measurement or VC measurement. The VC measurement quantifies the limit of a parallel classifier. The

VC measurement is characterized just like the biggest conceivable estimation of m for which there exists a preparation set of m diverse x focuses that the classifier can mark discretionarily.

Measuring the capacity of the model enables statistical learning hypothesis to make quantitative predictions. The most significant outcomes in the statistical learning hypothesis show that the inconsistency between training error and generalization error is limited from above by an amount that develops as the model capacity develops but shrinks as the quantity of training examples increases.

These limits give intellectual justification that the machine learning algorithm can work; however, they are rarely utilized when working with deep learning algorithms. This is in light of the fact that the limits are regularly free, and to some extent, it tends to be very hard to decide the limit of a deep learning algorithm. The issue of deciding the limit of a deep learning algorithm is particularly troublesome in light of the fact that the power limit is constrained by the abilities of the optimization algorithm, and we have a minimal theoretical understanding of the general non-curved optimization problem engaged with deep learning.

No Free Lunch Theorem

The machine learning algorithm claims that the learning algorithm can generalize well from a countless training set of examples. This particular claim of the machine learning algorithm seems to contradict some principles of logic. It is not logically valid to perform Inferring general rules and inductive reasoning from a limited set of examples. To logically set a rule describing every member of a set, it is compulsory to have knowledge about every member of that set.

Machine learning avoids this problem by offering probabilistic rules, rather than using certain rules on the basis of logical reasoning. Machine learning works on a promise of providing probably correct output. In terms of machine learning, the no free lunch theorem states that all data generating distributions, every algorithm has the same rate when classifying previously unobserved points. In simple words, no machine learning algorithm performs better than others.

Regularization

The no free lunch theorem suggests that we should develop our machine learning algorithms to perform well on the assigned tasks. This can be done by building preferences into the learning algorithm. At the point when these preferences are lined up with the learning algorithm, we request that the algorithm solve.

The only method for adjusting a learning algorithm that we have discussed is to increase or decrease the model's representational capacity by removing or adding functions from the hypothesis space of solutions from where the learning algorithm can choose. We gave a particular example of increasing or decreasing the level of a polynomial for a regression problem.

The conduct of our algorithm is strongly influenced not by how large we make the set of functions allowed in its hypothesis space, however by the particular identity of those capacities. The learning algorithm we have studied, like linear regression, has a hypothesis space comprising of the arrangement of straight elements. These linear functions can be very helpful for issues where the connection between inputs and outputs is genuinely linear. They are less valuable for issues that carry on in a nonlinear function. For instance, linear regression would not perform quite well if we attempted to utilize it to anticipate sin(x) from x. We can manage the performance of our algorithms by picking what sort of functions we enable them to draw solutions from, just by controlling the measure of these functions.

Hyperparameters and Validation Sets

Several settings option is given in the machine learning algorithm, which can be used to control the behavior of the algorithm. These settings are known as hyperparameters. The learning algorithm can't adopt the values of hyperparameters itself. (A nested learning procedure can be designed where one learning algorithm learns the best hyperparameters for another learning algorithm).

Cross-Validation

Dividing the entire dataset into the portion of a fixed training set or a fixed test set can bring problems as the test set being too small for applying tasks. A small test set suggests statistical uncertainty around the estimated test error, making it hard to guarantee that algorithm. A works better than algorithm B on the given task.

When the dataset has a huge number of examples, this isn't a major issue. When the dataset is excessively small, are alternative procedures allows one to utilize the examples in the estimation of the mean test error, at the cost of expanded computational cost? These methodologies depend on the idea of repeating the training and testing calculation on various arbitrarily chosen subsets or parts of the first dataset.

Estimators, Bias, and Variance

Statistical formulas provide different tools that can be used in the machine learning algorithm to solve a particular task not only on the training set but also on generalized. Basic concepts such as bias, parameter estimation, and variance are helpful to characterize notions of underfitting, overfitting, and generalization.

Point Estimation

Providing the only best prediction of some quantity of interest is known as point estimation.

Function Estimation

When performing function estimation through predicting a variable y given an input vector x.

Variance and Standard Error

This is another property of estimator, which indicates the amount of variation as a function in a data sample.

The variation or the standard error of an estimator gives a proportion of how we would expect the gauge we process from information to vary as we freely resample the dataset from the underlying information generating process. Similarly, as we might like an estimator to show low bias, we would like it to have generally low variance.

At the point when we figure any statistic utilizing a limited number of samples, our estimate of the genuine underlying parameter is uncertain, as we could have gotten different samples from a similar distribution, and their statistics would have been extraordinary.

Chapter 1

Explaining Supervised and Unsupervised Learning Algorithms

Supervised Learning Algorithms

Learning algorithm that is capable of learning and associating some input with some output from a given set of the training set of examples of inputs x and outputs y. In some cases, it is hard to collect the output y automatically and requires human supervision, but the term is still applicable even training set targets were automatically collected.

Probabilistic Supervised Learning

Supervised learning algorithms are based on estimating a probability distribution $p(y \mid x)$. This can be done by using the likelihood estimation to find the vector θ for distribution of parametric family $p(y \mid x; \theta)$.

Generalize linear regression to the classification scenario by characterizing a distinctive group of the probability distribution. For two classes, class 0 and class 1, we need to indicate the probability of one of these classes. The probability of class 1 decides the probability of class 0, as these two qualities must mean 1.

The ordinary distribution over real-valued numbers that we utilized for linear regression is parametrized as mean. A dispersion over a twofold factor is somewhat increasingly entangled, in light of the fact that its mean should consistently be somewhere in the range of 0 and 1.

Simple Supervised Learning Algorithms

Now quickly experience another non-probabilistic managed learning calculation, closest neighbor relapse. k - closest neighbors is a group of strategies that can be utilized for order or relapse. As a non-parametric learning calculation, k-closest neighbors aren't limited to a fixed number of parameters. We mostly think that the k-closest neighbor's calculation as not having any parameters, rather actualizing a basic capacity of the preparing information. In practice, there isn't even actually a preparation stage or learning process. Rather, at test time, when we need to deliver a yield y for another test input x, we discover the k-closest neighbors to x in the preparation information X. We at that point return the normal of the relating y esteems in the preparation set. This works for basically any sort of managed realizing where we can characterize a normal over y esteems. In the instance of the arrangement, we can average more than one-hot code vectors c with $c_y = 1$ what's more, $c_i = 0$ for every other estimation of I. We would then be able to decipher the normal over these one-hot codes as giving a likelihood circulation over classes. As a non-parametric learning calculation, k-closest neighbor can accomplish a high limit. For instance, assume we have a multiclass grouping assignment and measure execution with 0-1 misfortune. In this setting, 1-closest neighbor merges to twofold the Bayes blunder as the number of preparing models approaches interminability. The blunder in the overabundance of the Bayes mistake comes about because of picking a solitary neighbor by breaking ties between similarly far off neighbors. When there is unending preparing information, all test focuses x will have endlessly many preparing set neighbors at separation zero. When we permit the calculation to utilize these neighbors to cast a ballot, as opposed to arbitrarily picking one of them, the methodology merges to the Bayes mistake rate. The high limit of k-closest neighbors enables it to acquire high precision, given an enormous preparing set.

It operates at the high computational expense and giving small output, limited preparing set. One shortcoming of k-closest neighbors is that it can't discover that one component is more discriminative than another.

Unsupervised Learning Algorithms

The difference between supervised and unsupervised learning isn't officially and inflexibly characterized in light of the fact that there is no particular test for identifying whether a value is an element, or an objective given by an administrator. Unsupervised learning tries to extract data from a distribution that doesn't require human direction or supervision. The term is typically connected with density estimation, figuring out how to draw tests from a distribution, figuring out how to denoise information from some examples, finding a manifold that the information lies close, or bunching the information into sets of related models.

An exemplary unsupervised learning task is to locate the "best" representation of the information. By 'best,' we can mean various things, however, as a rule, we are looking for a representation that preserves however much data about x as could be expected while complying with some penalty or limitation planned for keeping the representation less complex or more open than x itself.

There are numerous methods for characterizing a simpler representation. Three of the most regular methods include lower-dimensional representation, sparse representation, and, lastly, independent representation. Low-dimensional representation attempts to pack much data about x as could reasonably be expected in a smaller representation. The utilization of sparse representation ordinarily requires expanding the dimensionality of the representation, with the goal that the representation turning out to generally zero doesn't dispose of an excess of data. This outcome in a general structure representation that will, in general, distribute data along the axes of the representation space. Independent representation attempts to disentangle the sources of variety hidden the information distribution with the end goal that the measurements of the representation are statistically independent.

Obviously, these three criteria are absolutely not mutually exclusive. Low dimensional representation regularly yields components that have less or more fragile conditions than the first high-dimensional data. This is a way to reduce the size of representation to discover and remove redundancies. Recognizing furthermore, expelling more excess permits the dimensionality decrease algorithm to accomplish more pressure while disposing of fewer data. The idea of representation is one of the focal subjects of deep learning, and along these lines, one of the focal subjects in this book.

K-Means Clustering

The k-implies dividing algorithm that separates the training set into k various groups of models that are close to one another. We would thus be able to think about the algorithm as giving a k-dimensional one-hot code vector h speaking to an information x. In the event that x has a place with a group I, at that point, hello there $= 1$ and every single other section of the representing h are zero.

The one-hot code gave by k-implies grouping is a case of a sparse representation, because most of its entrances are zero for each info. Afterward, we will create different calculations that adapt increasingly adaptable sparse representation, were beyond what one section can be non-zero for each information x. One-hot codes are an extraordinary case of sparse representation that loses a significant number of the advantages of a distributed representation. The one-hot code still presents some statistical advantages circumstances (it normally passes on the possibility that all models in a similar bunch are like one another), and it gives the preferred computational position that the whole representation might be caught by a single number.

The k-implies algorithm works by initializing k various centroids $\{\mu(1), \ldots, \mu(k)\}$ to various values, at that point switching back and forth between two distinct strides until assembly.

In one stage, each preparation model is allotted to bunch I, where I is the record of the closest centroid μ (i). In the other advance, every centroid $\mu(i)$ is refreshed to the mean of all preparation models x(j) allotted to the group I.

One trouble relating to clustering is that the grouping issue is naturally not well presented, as there is no single foundation that estimates how well a grouping of the information relates to this present reality. We can quantify properties of the grouping, for example, the normal Euclidean good ways from a cluster centroid to the individuals from the bunch. This enables us to advise how well we can remake the preparation information from the cluster assignments. We don't have the foggiest idea of how well the bunch assignments relate to the properties of this present reality. Besides, there might be a wide range of clustering that all relate well to some property of this present reality. We may want to discover a clustering that identifies with one element, however, get an alternate, similarly legitimate clustering that isn't important to our assignment. For example, assume that we run two clustering algorithms on a dataset comprising of pictures of red trucks, pictures of red vehicles, pictures of dim trucks, and pictures of dark vehicles. In the event that we request that each cluster calculation discover two groups, one calculation may discover a group of autos and a bunch of trucks, while another may discover a group of red vehicles and a group of dim vehicles. Assume we likewise run a third clustering algorithm, which is permitted to decide the number of groups. This may assign the guides to four clusters, red vehicles, red trucks, dim autos, and dark trucks. This new clustering now, in any event, catches data about the two characteristics; however, it has lost data about likeness. Red vehicles are in an alternate cluster from dim vehicles, similarly as they are in an alternate cluster from dim trucks. The yield of the clustering algorithm doesn't reveal to us that red vehicles are progressively like dim autos than they are to dim trucks. They are not quite the same as the two things, and that's it in a nutshell, we know.

These issues show a portion of the reasons that we may favor a distributed representation of a one-hot representation. A distributed representation could have two properties for every vehicle—one representing to its shading and one representing to regardless of whether it is a vehicle or a truck. It is as yet not so much clear what the ideal distributed representation is (in what capacity can the learning algorithm know whether the two characteristics we are keen on are shading and vehicle versus-truck as opposed to producer and age?) however having numerous traits diminishes the weight on the calculation to figure which single quality we care about, and enables us to gauge likeness between objects in a fine-grained path by looking at numerous characteristics rather than simply testing whether one quality matches.

Stochastic Gradient Descent

Stochastic Gradient Descent is an important algorithm that is powered in almost every deep learning algorithm. For good generalization, it is important to have large training sets of examples. The problem of having large training sets is that they are computationally more expensive.

Gradient descent has regularly been viewed as problematic and slow. In the past, the use of gradient descent enhance issues like optimization or becomes corrupt. Today, we realize that the machine learning models portrayed partially work very well when II prepared with gradient descent. The optimization algorithm may not be ensured to perform in a sensible measure of time, yet it regularly finds a very low value of the cost function rapidly enough to be valuable.

Stochastic gradient descent has numerous significant uses outside the setting of deep learning. It is the primary method to prepare enormous linear models on huge datasets. For a fixed model size, the expense per SGD update doesn't rely upon the preparing set size m. We frequently utilize a bigger model as the training set size increases; however, we are not compelled to do as such. The number of updates required to reach intermingling as a rule increment with training set size. As m draws near to infinity, the model will, in the long run, merge to its most ideal test mistake previously SGD has examined each model in the training set. Expanding m further won't expand the measure of training time expected to arrive at the model's most ideal test error.

Chapter 2

How to Design a
Machine Learning Algorithm

Designing a Machine Learning Algorithm

All deep learning algorithms are made up of a simple mixture of ingredients, such as combining a specification of a dataset, an optimization procedure, a model, and a cost function. For example, in linear regression algorithm dataset consists of combining x and y. By replacing any of the components independently, a variety of algorithms can be obtained.

There is at least one term available in the cost function that can help the learning process in performing statistical estimations. Negative log-likelihood is the most common cost function. To get maximum likelihood estimation, one has to minimize the cost function. Additional terms may be included in the cost function, such as regularization terms.

Motivational Factors of Deep Learning

The basic AI calculations discussed in this section work very well on a wide variety of significant issues. In any case, they have not prevailed with regards to comprehending the main issues in AI, for example, perceiving voice or perceiving objects. The improvement of deep learning was motivated partially by the disappointment of customary calculations to generalize well on such machine learning tasks.

This area is about how the test of generalizing to new models becomes increasingly troublesome when working with high-dimensional information, and how the systems used to accomplish generalization in conventional AI are deficient in learning confused capacities in high-dimensional spaces. Such spaces frequently force high computational expenses. Deep learning was intended to defeat these and different other challenges.

Problems with Dimensionality

When the number of dimensions in the data is high, it becomes highly difficult to resolve the problem arise during machine learning. This process is known as the curse of dimensionality. As the number of variables increases in the set, the problem of configuring these variables also increases.

Local Constancy and Smoothness Regularization

So as to generalize well, AI calculations should be guided by earlier instructions about what sort of capacity they ought to learn. Already, we have seen these priors joined as explicit instructions as a probability distribution over parameters of the model. We may talk about earlier beliefs as straightforwardly impacting itself and just in a roundabout way work following up on the parameters by means of their impact on the capacity. Also, we casually examine earlier beliefs as being communicated verifiably, by picking algorithms that are one-sided toward picking some class of functions over another, despite the fact that these bias may not be communicated (or on the other hand even conceivable to express) as far as a circulation speaking to our level of confidence in different capacities.

Among the most generally utilized of these certain "priors" is the smoothness prior to or local constancy prior. This prior express the capacity we learn not to change, especially inside a little area. Numerous less difficult algorithms depend solely on this before summing up well, and accordingly, they neglect to scale the factual difficulties engaged with tackling AI level assignments.

Another example of the local constancy approach is the k - nearest neighbor group of learning algorithms. These indicators are actually steady over each region containing every one of the point x that have a similar arrangement of k nearest neighbors in the preparation set. For k = 1, the number of recognizable districts can't be more than the quantity of preparing models. While the k - nearest neighbor's algorithm duplicates the yield from close by preparing models, most piece machines introduce between preparing set yields related to close by preparing models. A significant class of portions is the set of nearby portions where k(u, v) is huge when u = v and diminishes as u and v become more remote aside from one another. A nearby part can be thought of as a similitude work that performs layout coordinating, by estimating how firmly a test model x takes after each preparation model x(i).

Decision trees additionally experience the ill effects of the restrictions of solely smoothness-based learning since they break the information space into the same number of regions as there are leaves and utilize a different parameter (or here and there numerous parameters for expansions of decision trees) in every region. In the event that the target function requires a tree with at least n leaves to be spoken to precisely, at that point at any rate n preparing models are required to fit the tree. A numerous of n is expected to accomplish some level of factual trust in the anticipated yield. When all is said in done, to recognize O(k) districts in input space, these strategies require O(k) models. Ordinarily, there are O (k) parameters, with O(1) parameters.

Is there an approach to represent a complex function that has a lot more areas to be recognized than the quantity of preparing models? Unmistakably, accepting just smoothness of the basic capacity won't enable a student to do that. For instance, imagine that the objective capacity is a sort of checkerboard. A checkerboard contains numerous varieties, yet there is a straightforward structure to them. Imagine what happens when the quantity of preparing models is significantly littler than the quantity of highly contrasting squares on the checkerboard. Based on just local generalization and the smoothness or neighborhood consistency earlier, we would be ensured to effectively figure the shade of another point in the event that it exists in the equivalent checkerboard square as a training model. There is no assurance that the student could accurately stretch out the checkerboard example to focuses on lying in squares that do not contain training models.

The smoothness presumption and the related non-parametric learning algorithms work very well insofar as there are sufficient models for the learning algorithm to watch high focuses on most pinnacles and depressed spots on most valleys of the genuine hidden capacity to be scholarly. This is commonly evident when the capacity to be scholarly is smooth enough and shifts in hardly any enough measurements.

In high calculations, even a smooth capacity can change easily yet in a distinctive path along with each calculation. In the event that the capacity also acts in an unexpected way in various regions, it can turn out to be amazingly confounded to portray with a lot of training models. In the event that the capacity is convoluted (we need to recognize a large number of areas contrasted with the number of models), is there any plan to generalize well? The response to both of these inquiries—regardless of whether it is conceivable to speak to an entangled capacity productively, and whether it is workable for the assessed capacity to sum up well to new sources of info—is yes. The key understanding is that a huge number of districts, e.g., $O(2k)$, can be characterized with $O(k)$ models, so long as we present a few conditions between the districts through extra suppositions about the fundamental information creating circulation.

Different ways to deal with AI frequently make more grounded, task-explicit presumptions. For instance, we could, without much of a stretch, explain the checkerboard task by giving the supposition that the objective capacity is occasional. Normally we do exclude such solid, task-explicit suspicions into neural organizes so they can sum up to a lot wider variety of structures. Man-made intelligence tasks have a structure that is well complex to be constrained to straightforward, physically indicated properties, for example, periodicity, so we need learning algorithms that exemplify progressively broadly useful presumptions. The center thought in deep learning is that we expect that the information was created by the organization of components or highlights, conceivably at numerous levels in a chain of importance. Numerous other comparably conventional suppositions can additionally improve deep learning algorithms. These evidently gentle suppositions permit an exponential addition in the connection between the number of models and the number of areas that can be recognized.

Manifold Learning

A significant idea hidden numerous thoughts in AI is that of a complex. A complex is an associated locale. Numerically, it is a lot of focuses, related to an area around each point. From some random point, the complex locally has all the earmarks of being a Euclidean space. In regular day to day existence, we experience the outside of the world as a 2-D plane; however, it is in actuality around complex in 3-D space. The meaning of an area encompassing each point suggests the presence of changes that can be applied to proceed onward the complex from one position to a neighboring one. In the case of the world's surface as a complex, one can walk north, south, east, or west.

In spite of the fact that there is formal numerical importance to the expression "complex," in AI it will, in general, be utilized all the more freely to assign an associated set of focuses that can be approximated well by considering just a few degrees of opportunity, or measurements, implanted in a higher-dimensional space. Each measurement compares to a nearby course of variety. Many AI issues appear to be miserable in the event that we anticipate the machine learning calculation to learn capacities with fascinating varieties over the entirety of Rn.

Complex learning calculations surmount this hindrance by accepting that most of Rn comprise of invalid data sources, and that fascinating information sources happen just along an assortment of manifolds containing a little subset of focuses, with intriguing varieties in the yield of the scholarly capacity happening just along headings that lie on the complex, or with intriguing varieties happening just when we move starting with one complex then onto the next. Complex learning was presented for the situation of constant esteemed information and the unaided picking upsetting, despite the fact that this likelihood fixation thought can be summed up to both discrete information and the directed getting the hang of setting: the key suspicion remains that likelihood mass is exceptionally thought.

The suspicion that the information lies along a low-dimensional complex may not continuously be right or helpful. We contend that with regards to AI undertakings, for example, those that include handling pictures, sounds, or content, the complex supposition that is in any event around right. The proof for this supposition comprises of two classes of perceptions.

Chapter 3

Basic of Deep Feedforward Networks

Deep feedforward networks are also known as feedforward neural networks or multiplayer perceptrons (MLPs), are the best quality deep learning models. The purpose of this network is to approximate some function "f."

These models are called feedforward in light of the fact that data courses through the work being assessed from x, through the halfway calculations used to characterize f, lastly to the output y. There are no input associations wherein outputs of the model are sustained once again into itself. When feedforward neural systems are reached out to incorporate feedback connections, they are called recurrent neural networks.

Feedforward systems are crucial to machine learning experts. They structure the premise of numerous significant business applications. For instance, the convolutional systems utilized for object acknowledgment from photographs are a concentrated sort of feedforward organize. Feedforward systems are a theoretical venturing stone on the way to recurrent systems, which control numerous normal language applications.

Feedforward neural networks are called networks since they are incorporated by composing together a wide range of functions. The model is related to a coordinated non-cyclic chart depicting how the functions are made together. For instance, we may have three functions f (1), f (2), and f (3) associated in a chain, to shape f(x) = f(3)(f (2)(f(1) (x))). These chain structures are the most usually utilized structures of neural systems. For this situation, f (1) is known as the first layer of the system, f (2) is known as the subsequent layer, etc. The general length of the chain gives the profundity of the model. It is from this wording the name "deep learning" emerges. The last layer of a feedforward arrange is called the output layer. During neural system preparing, we drive f(x) to coordinate f∗(x). The preparation information gives us noisy, rough instances of f ∗(x) assessed at various preparing focuses. Every model x is joined by a name y ≈ f ∗(x). The preparation models determine straightforwardly what the yield layer must do at each point x; it must deliver a worth that is near y. The conduct of different layers is not legitimately indicated by the preparation information. The learning calculation must choose instructions to utilize those layers to deliver the ideal yield, yet the preparation information does not state what every individual layer ought to do. Rather, the learning calculation must choose how to utilize these layers to execute an estimation of f best∗. Since the preparation information doesn't show the ideal yield for every one of these layers, these layers are called concealed layers.

At long last, these systems are called neural in light of the fact that they are approximately propelled by neuroscience. Each shrouded layer of the system is commonly vector-esteemed. The dimensionality of these concealed layers decides the width of the model. Each component of the vector might be deciphered as assuming a job similar to a neuron. Instead of thinking about the layer as speaking to a solitary vector-to-vector work, we can likewise think about the layer as comprising of numerous units that demonstration in parallel, each speaking to a vector-to-scalar work. Every unit takes after a neuron in the feeling that it gets a contribution from numerous different units and registers its own initiation esteem. Using numerous layers of vector-esteemed portrayal is drawn from neuroscience.

It is ideal to consider feedforward arranges as capacity estimate machines that are intended to accomplish measurable speculation, sporadically drawing a few bits of knowledge from what we think about the mind, as opposed to as models of cerebrum work. One approach to comprehend feedforward systems is in the first place direct models, what's more, think about how to conquer their impediments. Straight models, for example, calculated relapse and straight relapse, are engaging on the grounds that they might be fit proficiently what's more, dependably, either in shut structure or with curved streamlining. Straight models, moreover, have the undeniable imperfection that the model limit is constrained to straight works, so the model can't comprehend the collaboration between any two info factors.

Tips for choosing to map.

- One alternative is to utilize a very conventional φ, for example, the unbounded dimensional φ that is certainly utilized by portion machines dependent on the RBF bit. In the event that $\varphi(x)$ is of sufficiently high measurement, we can generally have enough ability to fit the preparing set, yet speculation to the test set regularly stays poor. Very conventional include mappings are generally founded uniquely on the standard of nearby smoothness and don't encode enough earlier data to settle progressed issues.

- Another alternative is to design φ physically. Until the appearance of profound learning, this was the prevailing methodology. This methodology requires many years of human exertion for each different undertaking, with professionals having some expertise in various areas, for example, discourse acknowledgment or PC vision, and with a little movement between spaces.

- The system of profound learning is to learn φ. In this methodology, we have a model $y = f(x;\theta,w) = \varphi(x; \theta)\square w$. We presently have parameters θ that we use to learn φ from an expansive class of capacities, and parameters w that guide from $\varphi(x)$ to the ideal yield. This is a case of a profound feedforward arrange, with φ characterizing a shrouded layer. This methodology is just one of the three that abandons the convexity of the preparation issue; however, the advantages exceed the damages. In this methodology, we parametrize the portrayal as $\varphi(x; \theta)$ what's more, utilize the advancement calculation to discover the θ

that compares to a decent portrayal. In the event that we wish, this methodology can catch the advantage of the first approach by being exceptionally nonexclusive—we do as such by utilizing an extremely expansive family$\varphi(x; \theta)$. This methodology can likewise catch the advantage of the subsequent methodology. Human specialists can encode their insight to help speculation by structuring families $\varphi(x; \theta)$ that they expect will perform well. The preferred position is that the human fashioner just needs to locate the correct general capacity family instead of finding exactly the correct capacity.

This general guideline of improving models by learning highlights stretches out past the feedforward systems depicted in this part. It is a repetitive topic of profound discovering that applies to the entirety of the sorts of models portrayed all through this book. Feedforward systems are the utilization of this rule to learning deterministic mappings from x to y that need criticism associations. Different models exhibited later will apply these standards to learning stochastic mappings, learning capacities with input, and learning likelihood appropriations over a solitary vector. We start this section with a basic case of a feedforward arrange. Next, we address every one of the structure choices expected to convey a feedforward organize.

To start with, preparing a feedforward to organize requires making a significant number of similar structure choices as are fundamental for a direct model: picking the analyzer, the expense work, and the type of the yield units. We survey these nuts and bolts of inclination based adapting, at that point, continue to face a portion of the structure choices that are remarkable to feedforward systems. Feedforward systems have presented the idea of a concealed layer, and this expects us to pick the enactment capacities that will be utilized to register the shrouded layer esteems. We should likewise plan the engineering of the system, including what number of layers the system ought to contain, how these layers ought to be associated with one another, and what number of units ought to be in each layer. Learning in profound neural systems requires processing the slopes of confused capacities. We present the back-spread calculation and its current speculations, which can be utilized to figure these slopes effectively. At last, we close with some authentic viewpoint.

Gradient-Based Learning

Planning and preparing a neural system isn't entirely different from preparing any other AI model with gradient descent. The biggest distinction between the linear models we have seen up until this point and neural systems is that the nonlinearity of a neural system causes most interesting loss functions to become non-convex. This means neural systems are for the most part prepared by utilizing iterative, angle based enhancers that only drive the cost function to an exceptionally low value, instead of the direct condition solvers used to prepare linear equation models or the curved linear regression with worldwide assembly ensures used to prepare calculated relapse or SVMs. Convex optimization beginning from any underlying parameters (in principle—it is very powerful yet can experience numerical issues). Stochastic gradient descent applied to non-convex loss functions has no such convergence assurance, and is delicate to the estimations of the underlying parameters. For feedforward neural systems, it is critical to instate all loads to little arbitrary qualities. The predispositions might be instated to zero or too little positive qualities.

We can obviously, train models, for example, linear regression and support vector machines with gradient descent as well, and in reality, when the training set is very large. Starting here of view, training a neural system isn't vastly different from training some other model. Processing the gradient is complicated for a neural system; however, it should, in any case, be possible productively and precisely. Similarly, as with other AI models, to apply gradient-based learning, we must pick a cost function, and we should pick how to speak to the output of the model. We currently return to these structure considerations with special emphasis on the situation of the neural system.

Cost Function

A significant part of the plan of a deep neural system is the decision of the cost function. Luckily, the cost functions for neural systems are pretty much equivalent to those for other parametric models, for example, linear models. Much of the time, our parametric model characterizes a distribution $p(y \mid x;\theta)$, and we basically utilize the rule of maximum probability. This implies we utilize the cross-entropy between the training data and the model's expectations as the cost function.

At times, we adopt a less difficult strategy, where instead of foreseeing a complete probability over y, we just anticipate some measurement of y molded on x. Specific loss functions enable us to prepare an indicator of these assessments. The absolute cost function used to prepare a neural system will frequently consolidate one of the essential cost functions depicted here with a regularization term.

Chapter 4

Machine Learning for the Future

Many applications and machines use deep learning nowadays. The concepts of machine learning and deep learning are in their basic stage, and there is a lot of room for improvement. Scientists who are planning for the future see a lot of advancement in this field and are looking for different ways to incorporate machine learning in our daily lives. Deep learning is used in many applications and performs its function quite well. In this chapter, we will look at the applications of deep learning; and how it can help the scientists create solutions that can help us perform our daily tasks.

One of the basic issues with machine learning is that it will reduce human effort and may stop people from working in the near future. On the contrary, deep learning is helping people complete day-to-day tasks with ease. From flipping burgers in the restaurants to creating sophisticated machines, deep learning has enhanced people's thinking and giving us an interesting way to complete our tasks. You also need to understand that new jobs created by deep learning will also require additional knowledge and training.

Every new technology introduced in the world has its pitfalls. The new issues raised by the machine and deep learning needs to be taken seriously. Technology is in its infant form, and we do not know where it will lead us.

New Technology for the Future

Technology needs to prove itself if it needs to be accepted by people. The new technologies need to compete with the existing tech and prove to be monetary stability as well. It should provide essential insight and has a scalable structure. Machine learning solved many problems that were faced by the earlier machines. With their adaptable interfaces, they can solve the problems easily. Old machines faced many issues regarding problem-solving and were incapable of learning from their mistakes. Deep Machine learning needs to adhere to the hard-core functionalities if it needs to be accepted by people all over the world. The technology needs to be in the mainstream so that all the people can use it. In the next section, we will discuss the future of machine learning and – and what makes the deep learning a concept that everyone can back.

Deep Machine Learning for Robotics

Robots in the future need to cater to real-world problems and solve them faster than human beings. When talking about robots, you might draw a connection of some robot you saw in cartoons or movies. To attract the attention of the public, a robot must adhere to some hardcore rules and perform some tasks. Deep machine learning enables robots to tackle problems in an effective manner and solve more than one problem. Technology needs to have a large number of followers if it needs to be accepted by the world. We do not want a world of deadly robots, so scientists are carefully treading in this department and making robots than can complete basic tasks such as cleaning, computing, and making food.

Roomba is one of the best examples of early computing and deep learning. It has attracted a lot of attention and has a huge fan following. This robot can work at the commercial and home level. This is merely a fancy vacuum cleaner and has a simple and effective algorithm. With the help of these algorithms, the Roomba can easily navigate in the house. This task may seem very easy, but it requires a complex code. The Roomba robot needs to be cleaned when it's full, and in the near future, you can expect that the vacuum cleaner will also clean itself, and all this will be achieved by complex code and deep learning.

Apart from Roomba, many robots help us in our daily lives. Not all are available for commercial use and are in their production phase. Nowadays, robots only perform a special task and prove to be a general helped in our daily tasks. With deep learning, you will see that robots will become a major part of our daily lives.

Machine Learning in Health Care

Elderly care is one of the main departments, where machine learning has done wonders. People who live in nursing homes do not have many things to do in their last years, and with deep machines, learning robots help them to spend their time at home and create a safe environment for them. There are many countries that have a shortage of elderly care workers, and these robots prove to be a viable alternative. Due to this, many countries are spending a humongous sum to solve the problems faced by robots. The telepresence robot is one of the tech marvels that can be seen in nursing homes. This robot is perfect for places with fewer doctors. These robots will help the doctors to hear and see the patients and cater to their problems.

In the health care department, robotics has been making constant strides. In the near future, you can expect the robots to complete the surgeries with precision and diagnose the patients. This will decrease the reliance on the doctors, and we will be able to eliminate human errors from the medical field.

Deep Machine Learning for Smart Systems

Different machines are currently assisting humans in performing their work effectively. They complete tasks effectively, but they are not usually designed to complete a diverse set of tasks. They complete the same task repeatedly. An application can help you to find the restaurant in an effective manner and can book a table for you in a short time. You do not need to make a call to book a restaurant as the machine learning adapts to your needs and mimics the basic human intelligence to communicate with real people for you. With the help of deep learning, the machines learn the likes, dislike of the people, and increase their decision-making capabilities.

Machine Learning for Industries

Efficiently is the focus of the robots and machines used in industrial settings. The main reason behind using the robots is that they complete the tasks in an effective manner and also save time in the process. This helps the organization to save both money and resources. This also reduces the reliance on human beings and minimize human errors. Machine learning is used in different industrial settings such as data mining, speed recognition, product categorization, bioinformatics, medical diagnostics, and information retrieval. This is just a basic list of the solutions provided by the machines at this age. With advanced algorithms and understanding of deep learning, there is an increased chance that the machines will take over basic human jobs in the industries. In a generalized industrial setting, machine learning provides help in many sectors, such as:

Analyzation: Understanding customer behavior such as why and when the user wants to make a purchase. What are the basic response of the users and how to categorize their responses!

Adaptation: with the help of adaption strategies employed by the robots, the user will get customized experiences when they interact with your system. This increases productivity and reduces frustration.

Control: With the help of deep learning, the machines can steer the customers in the right manner and increase the probability of success.

Optimization: With optimization techniques, the modification of the environment happens, and it helps to utilize the resources in a better fashion.

Enrichment: Automatic addition of the ads and widgets in the environment that can increase the user experience and help the company to improve sales.

Understanding how the machine works in the industrial setting is good, but you need to understand its application in our lives as well. Machine learning is an important aspect of our daily lives and can help us complete many tasks with ease. Many online applications and programs rely on machine learning to create an exceptional experience for users. Machine learning helps us to predict heart strokes, identifying different diseases, and automating the employees' access to companies. Different companies spend millions on improving the working of computers and applications to bring ease in their lives and to increase productivity.

Finding New Work Opportunities with Machine Learning

You can discover in excess of a couple of articles that talk about the loss of employments that AI and its related advancements will cause. Robots, as of now, play out various undertakings that used to utilize people, and this utilization will increment after some time. The previous segment of this section supported you in seeing a portion of the down to earth, genuine uses for AI today and helped you dis-spread where those utilizations are probably going to extend later on. While perusing this segment, you should have additionally thought about how those new uses might cost you or a friend or family member a vocation. A few creators have ventured to such an extreme as to state that the future may hold a situation were adapting new aptitudes probably won't ensure a vocation.

The truth is that choosing exactly how AI will influence the workplace is hard, similarly as it was difficult for individuals to see where the mechanical upheaval would take us in the method for mass-delivering products for the general buyer. Similarly, as those laborers expected to secure new positions, so individuals confronting the loss of occupation to AI today should secure new positions.

Working for a Machine

It's completely conceivable that you'll wind up working for a machine later on. Truth be told, you may as of now work for a machine and not know it. A few organizations, as of now, use AI to break down business procedures and make them progressively effective. For instance, Hitachi right now uses such an arrangement in central administration. For this situation, the AI really gives the work orders dependent on its investigation of the work process — similarly as a human center supervisor may do. The thing that matters is that the AI is really eight percent more proficient than the people it replaces. For another situation, Amazon ran a challenge among AI specialists to make sense of whether the organization could all the more likely procedure representative approval forms, consequently utilizing AI. Once more, the fact was to make sense of how to supplant center administration and cut a touch of the formality.

Be that as it may, an opening for work additionally introduces itself. Laborers under the AI do play out the undertakings that the AI instructs them to do, yet they can utilize their own understanding and innovativeness in deciding how to play out the assignment. The

AI breaks down the procedures that the human specialists use and measures the outcomes accomplished. Any fruitful procedures get included in the database of strategies that laborers can apply to achieve assignments. At the end of the day, the people are showing the AI new strategies to make the workplace considerably progressively productive.

This is a case of how AI can liberate people from the drudgery of the workplace. When utilizing human center chiefs, new procedures frequently get covered in an administration of implicit guidelines and inner self. The AI center supervisor is intended to adapt new methods without inclination, so the people are urged to practice their innovativeness, and everybody benefits. So, the AI, which does not have an inner self to wound, is the receptive administrator that numerous specialists have needed from the beginning.

Working with Machines

Individuals, as of now, work with machines all the time — they may just not understand it. For instance, when you converse with your cell phone, and it perceives what you state, you're working with a machine to accomplish an ideal objective. A great many people perceive that the voice collaboration gave a cell phone improves with time — the more you use it, the better it gets at perceiving your voice. As the student calculation turns out to be better tuned, it turns out to be increasingly effective at perceiving your voice and acquiring the ideal outcome. This pattern will proceed.

Nonetheless, AI is utilized in a wide range of ways that probably won't jump out at you. At the point when you point a camera at a subject, and the camera can put a container around the face (to help focus on the image), you see the aftereffect of AI. The camera is helping you play out the activity of snapping a photo with far more prominent effectiveness. Also, the camera naturally expels probably a portion of the impacts of shaking and terrible lighting. Cameras have gotten very great at helping people to perform errands easily.

The utilization of decisive dialects, for example, SQL (Structured Query Language), will turn out to be progressively articulated also on the grounds that AI will make advancements conceivable. In certain regards, an explanatory language essentially gives you a chance to portray what you need and not how to get it. In any case, SQL still requires a PC researcher, information researcher, database executive, or some other expert to utilize. Future dialects won't have this impediment. In the long run, somebody who is prepared to play out a specific errand well will basically guide the robot colleague, and the robot aide will find the way to do it. People will utilize imagination to find what to do; the subtleties (the by what means) will turn into the space of machines.

Fixing Machines

A large portion of this section talks about current innovation, where the innovation will go later on, and why things fill in as they do. Be that as it may see that the talk consistently centers on the innovation accomplishing something. It's hard to believe, but it's true before the innovation can do whatever else, it must play out a commonsense assignment that will stand out and advantage people in a way that makes individuals need to have the innovation for their own. It doesn't make a difference what the innovation is. In the end, innovation will break. Getting the innovation to accomplish something valuable is the prime thought now, and the finish of any fantasies of what the innovation will, in the long run, do extends a long time into the future, such commonplace things like fixing the innovation will, in any case, fall on human shoulders. Regardless of whether the human isn't straightforwardly engaged with the physical fix, human insight will coordinate the fixed activity.

A few articles that you read online may cause you to accept that self-fixing robots are, as of now, a reality. For instance, the International Space Station robots, Dextre and Canadarm, played out a fix of a defective camera. What the tales don't state is that a human chose how to play out the assignment and guided the robots to do the physical work. The self-governing fix is preposterous, with the calculations accessible today. Fixes regularly beset human specialists, and until robots duplicate the information and abilities of these specialists, similar fixes will stay unthinkable for them.

Making New AI Errands

AI calculations aren't inventive, which implies that people must give the inventiveness that improves AI. Indeed, even calculations that manufacture different calculations just improve the effectiveness and precision of the outcomes that the calculation accomplishes — they can't make calculations that perform new sorts of errands. People must make a vital contribution to characterizing these assignments and the procedures expected to start unraveling them.

You may feel that lone specialists in AI will make new AI errands. Nonetheless, the tale about the center chief from Hitachi dis-cussed in the "Working for a machine" area, prior in this part, should disclose to you that things will work uniquely in contrast to that. Truly, specialists will help structure the reason for characterizing how to settle the assignment; however, the genuine production of errands will originate from individuals who realize a specific industry best. The Hitachi story fills in as a reason for understanding both that the future will see individuals from varying backgrounds contributing toward AI situations and that a particular instruction probably won't help in characterizing new undertakings.

Concocting New AI Conditions

Right now, concocting new AI conditions is the domain of innovative work organizations. A gathering of profoundly prepared masters must make the parameters for another condition. For instance, NASA needs robots to investigate Mars. For this situation, NASA relies on the abilities of individuals at MIT and Northeastern to play out the assignment. Given that the robot should perform errands self-ruling, the AI calculations will turn out to be very mind-boggling and incorporate a few levels of critical thinking.

In the long run, somebody will have the option to depict an issue in adequate detail that a particular program can make an important calculation utilizing a suitable language. As such, normal individuals will, in the end, start making new AI situations dependent on thoughts they have and need to attempt. As with making AI undertakings, individuals who make future situations will be specialists in their specific specialty, as opposed to being PC researchers or information scientists. Fathoming the study of AI will, in the long run, transform into an engineering exercise that will give anybody with a smart thought the necessary access.

Staying away from the Potential Pitfalls of Future Technologies

Any new innovation accompanies potential traps. The higher the desires for that innovation, the more extreme the traps become. Unreasonable desires cause a wide range of issues with AI since individuals believe that what they find in motion pictures is the thing that they'll get in reality. It's fundamental to recall the essential ideas— that AI calculations as of now can't feel, think autonomously, or make anything. In contrast to those film AIs, an AI calculation does correctly what you anticipate that it should do, that's it. Obviously, a portion of the outcomes are stunning; however, keeping desires in accordance with what genuine innovation can do is significant. Else, you'll guarantee something that the innovation can never convey, and those disciples whom you were expecting will go searching for the following huge thing.

Truth be told, the utilizations for AI today are very tight. The machine can't deduce anything, which restrains the utilization of the machine to the undertaking for which the engineer or information researcher structured it. Actually, a great relationship for the present calculations is that they're similar to a customized shirt. You need particular aptitudes to make a calculation that is custom-made to address explicit issues today; however, the future could see calculations that can handle almost any errand. Companies that depend on thin AI need to practice care by the way they create items or administrations. An adjustment in an item or administration contributions may put the information utilized for the AI condition outside the student calculation's space, lessening the yield of the AI calculation to jabber (or possibly making it questionable).

Deep Machine learning, a method that enables the machine to pick contributions by utilizing multiple preparing layers to investigate complex structures, is the subsequent stage in the process of utilizing AI in reasonable ways; however, barely any organizations at present utilize it, and it requires a colossal measure of processing capacity to perform handy errands. The Deep Learning furnishes you with assets for working with profound learning in the event that you need to do as such. This site offers articles, instructional exercises, model code, and other data that you have to see profound adapting better. Despite the fact that you may feel that everybody utilizes profound adapting today, it's really a future innovation that a couple of organizations decide to grasp despite the fact that it isn't idealized (or anyplace close to consummated) now.

Utilizing AI in an association additionally necessitates that you contract individuals with the correct arrangement of aptitudes and make a group. AI in the corporate environment, where results mean an improvement in the main concern, is generally new. Organizations face difficulties in getting the correct group together, building up a sensible arrangement of objectives, and afterward really achieving those objectives. To draw in a world-class group, your organization brings to the table an issue that is energizing enough to lure the individuals required from different associations is anything but a simple errand, and you have to consider it part of characterizing the objectives for making an AI domain.

Chapter 5

Regulations for Deep Learning

There are some rules that need to be followed when the developers are working on deep learning. One of the main problems that are faced by machine learning coders is how to ensure that the algorithm performs well on the training data and the inputs. The coders to ensure the reduction of error use many strategies. This results in facing different issues in training. In this chapter, we will discuss the different regulation strategies implied by the deep learning practitioner.

The regularizing estimators pave the way for the regularization strategies of deep learning. A good regularizer will not consider much bias and will have a reduced variance. Deep learning algorithms will take the general data from outside the model family, and to analyze the data, the machines need to learn the process of categorizing the data, and the regulations help in this scenario. Complexity is inevitable when it comes to machine learning. Controlling the complexity is not the process of finding the right size and right parameters for the model family – it generally ensures finding the best-suited model that could be regularized appropriately. Look into parameter norm penalties that can help to garner the needs of the deep and regularized model.

Parameter Norm Penalties

The parameters have been in the IT world long before the introduction of machine learning. The simple and effective regulation strategies such as linear regression and logistic regression have paved the way for more advanced parameters such as linear network regression and parameter norm penalty. When there is a reduction in the training algorithm, you will also see a reduction in the original objective and the size of the parameter. Different sizes of the parameter norm will result in different result options. We will discuss the effects of different norms when the model parameter penalties are used.

When you are working on the neural networks, it is recommended that you use a different penalty coefficient for different layers of the network. The search space can be reduced when you use the same weight decay, as this will reduce the size of the search.

Constrained Optimization as Norm Penalties

When we construct the generalized Lagrange function, we can easily minimize the function subjects. The Lagrange function usually consists of a different set of penalties and the original objective function. The penalties are the product of the function that represents whether the constraint is satisfied, and the coefficient called KKT multiplier. In the neural networks and deep machine learning, we also use explicit constraints instead of penalties. The algorithm can be modified by changing the penalty parameters, and this will help the machine understand when to change the course of action. With fewer data to analyze, the machine will take less time to search for the alpha value. The constrained optimization ensures that the machines learn and dwell on the limited power and become more advanced. This concept helped many companies ensure that computers can learn from their experiences and provide viable computing solutions.

Regulation of Under-Constrained Problems

In many cases of computing, it is essential that the problems be clearly defined. When you are working on linear models of machine learning, the matrix needs to be inverted to observe the variance. You may find that the variance is defined in the same direction because there are fewer examples of input features. When you do not have enough data in the matrix, it is possible that the solution is underdetermined. Perfect classification of data is essential when you are looking to solve under-constrained problems. Many regulations can help to solve the problems in a proficient manner. The regularizations for solving the problems are a very complicated process, and researchers are still working on finding new ways to cater to the needs of under-constrained problems.

Dataset Augmentation

The ideal approach to make an AI model sum up better is to prepare it on more information. Obviously, by and by, the measure of information we have is constrained. One approach to get around this issue is to make counterfeit information and add it to the preparation set. For some AI errands, it is sensibly direct to make new phony information.

This methodology isn't as promptly as material to numerous different undertakings. For instance, it is difficult to produce new phony information for a thickness estimation task except if we have just tackled the thickness estimation issue.

Dataset augmentation has been an especially effective procedure for a specific classification issue: object acknowledgment. Pictures are high dimensional and incorporate a gigantic assortment of elements of variety, a considerable lot of which can be effectively reenacted. Activities like deciphering the preparation pictures a couple of pixels toward every path can frequently significantly improve speculation, regardless of whether the model has just been intended to be mostly interpretation invariant by utilizing the convolution and pooling systems. Numerous different activities, for example, pivoting the picture or scaling the picture, have additionally demonstrated very effective.

One must be mindful so as not to apply changes that would change the right class. For instance, optical character acknowledgment assignments require perceiving the difference between 'b' and 'd' and the difference somewhere in the range of '6' and '9', so even flips and 180° pivots are not fitting methods for increasing datasets for these undertakings.

There are likewise changes that we might want our classifiers to be invariant to, yet which are difficult to perform. For instance, the out-of-plane revolution cannot be actualized as a straightforward geometric activity on the info pixels. Dataset augmentation is effective for discourse acknowledgment undertakings also.

Infusing clamor in the contribution to a neural system can likewise be viewed as a type of information augmentation. For some classification and even some relapse errands, the undertaking should, at present, be conceivable to illuminate regardless of whether little irregular commotion is added to the information. Neural systems demonstrate not to be very strong to clamor, be that as it may (Tang and Eliasmith, 2010). One approach to improve the strength of neural systems is just to prepare them with arbitrary commotion applied to their data sources. Information commotion infusion is a piece of some solo learning calculations; for example, the denoising autoencoder (Vincent et al., 2008). Commotion infusion additionally works when the clamor is applied to the concealed units, which can be viewed as doing dataset augmentation at different degrees of deliberation.

When looking at AI benchmark results, it is essential to consider the effect of dataset augmentation. Frequently, hand-structured dataset augmentation plans can significantly lessen the speculation blunder of an AI strategy. To look at the exhibition of one AI calculation to another, it is important to perform controlled investigations. When looking at AI calculation An and AI calculation B, it is important to ensure that the two calculations were assessed utilizing a similar hand-structured dataset augmentation plans. Assume that calculation A performs inadequately with no dataset augmentation, and calculation B performs well when joined with various manufactured changes of the information. In such a case, it is likely the engineered changes caused the improved presentation, as opposed to the utilization of AI calculation B. In some cases choosing whether analysis has been appropriately controlled requires emotional judgment. For instance, AI calculations that infuse commotion into the information are playing out a type of dataset augmentation. Ordinarily, tasks that are commonly relevant, (for example, adding Gaussian clamor to the info) are viewed as a component of the AI calculation, while activities that are specific to one application area, (for example, haphazardly trimming a picture) are viewed as isolated pre-handling steps.

You need to make sure that you also learn the concept pf early stopping when you need to acquaint yourself with the concept of deep learning. You will learn about the optimization of deep models in the next chapter that will give you a clear understanding of this subject.

Chapter 6

Optimization of Deep Models

When you are working in a deep learning genre, there are many optimization strategies. Different optimization strategies are used to write and design algorithms that are used by the machines. Developers may spend months on developing a single algorithm to solve a basic problem. The optimization of the algorithm is essential to ensure that the problem is solved in a timely fashion. These optimization techniques ensure that the problems are catered to in an effective manner. Some optimization techniques used in the neural networks are discussed in this chapter. Learn about the gradient-based optimization to get a clear understanding of the optimization techniques used in neural networks. First, we will discuss finding the parameters that reduce the cost function. This includes the performance measure of the entire data set as well as different regularization terms. You need to understand that pure optimization is different from training optimization when it comes to machine learning. The next section will focus on providing information on this topic:

Pure Optimization vs. Learning Optimization

There are many differences in pure optimization and training optimization. Machine learning is an indirect method. In machine learning, our focus is to find the performance measures that are defined with the help of test data. This test data will not always help to find the right solution as the data might differ in the real world scenario. In the training optimization, the cost function is reduced to find the right values, and this cannot be done in pure optimization. In pure optimization, our main goal is to reduce the cost function, and we need to derive the algorithm that can help us achieve this. You need to learn about the formulas and concepts of empirical risk minimization, early stopping, surrogate loss functions, and batch algorithms to understand the vast differences between pure and learning optimization.

Challenges Faced In Neural Network Optimization

Optimization for the neural networks and machines is a very daunting task. The machine learning has minimized the difficulties of the optimization by ensuring that the objective functions and constraints are carefully designed. When you need to study the optimization of the neural networks, you need to presume that the optimization problem is non-convex. You will learn about the common challenges that are faced during the optimization of the neural networks. One of the most prominent challenges that you will face when optimizing the convex functions is ill-conditioning. You will face this problem when you are optimizing the numerical, convex, and non-convex functions. This problem is present in the neural network training, and this problem is caused when the SGD is stuck.

It presumes that small changes will drastically increase the cost function. Ill-conditioning also occurs in different settings, but the solutions are not generally applicable to neural networks. Local Minima is another prominent issue that you will have to face when optimizing the neural networks. The local minimum is considered a global minimum, and when you are optimizing the convex functions, you will know that you have found a good solution when you find a critical point. Some other challenges that you will have to face during the neural network optimization are saddle points and flat regions, exploding gradients, long-term dependencies, inexact gradients, and the theoretical limit of optimization.

Basic Algorithms of Optimization

Stochastic gradient descent is one of the most used algorithms in deep machine learning and is also used in machine learning. With the help of this algorithm, you can find the unbiased estimate of the gradient.

A significant parameter for the SGD calculation is the learning rate. Beforehand, we have depicted SGD as utilizing a fixed learning rate. By and by, it is important to diminish the learning rate after some time slowly, so we presently indicate the learning rate at cycle.

This is on the grounds that the SGD slope estimator presents a wellspring of clamor (the arbitrary inspecting of m preparing models) that doesn't disappear in any event, when we land at any rate. By examination, the genuine inclination of the absolute cost work turns out to be little and afterward 0 when we approach and arrive at any rate utilizing cluster angle plummet, so a bunch slope plunge can utilize a fixed learning rate.

The most significant property of SGD and related minibatch or online inclination based streamlining is that calculation time per update doesn't develop with the quantity of preparing models. This permits assembly in any event when the quantity of preparing models turns out to be huge. For a huge enough dataset, SGD may unite to inside some fixed resilience of its final test set mistake before it has handled the whole preparing set.

While stochastic angle plunge stays a mainstream improvement procedure, learning with it can here, and there be moderate. The technique for energy (Polyak, 1964) is intended to quicken adapting, particularly even with high ebb and flow little yet steady inclinations, or loud angles. The energy calculation amasses an exponentially rotting moving normal of past slopes and keeps on moving toward them.

Officially, the force calculation presents a variable v that assumes the job of speed—it is the bearing and speed at which the parameters travel through parameter space. The speed is set to an exponentially rotting normal of the negative angle. The name energy gets from a physical relationship, where the negative inclination is a power moving a molecule through parameter space, as per Newton's laws of motion. The energy in material science is mass occasions speed. In the energy learning calculation, we accept unit mass, so the speed vectors may likewise be viewed as the force of the molecule.

Parameter Initialization Strategies

Some enhancement calculations are not iterative commonly and just explain for an answer point. Other advancement calculations are iterative essentially in any case, when applied to the correct class of enhancement issues, meet to worthy arrangements in a satisfactory measure of time paying little respect to instatement. Profound picking up preparing calculations, as a rule, don't have both of these extravagances. Preparing calculations for profound learning models is generally iterative in nature and in this way, requires the client to determine some underlying point from which to start the emphasis. Besides, preparing profound models is a sufficiently difficult task that most calculations are firmly affected by the decision of instatement. The underlying point can decide if the calculation combines by any means, with some underlying focuses being shaky to the point that the calculation experiences numerical difficulties and flops through and through. When learning converges, the underlying point can decide how rapidly learning combines and whether it merges to a point with high or minimal effort. Likewise, purposes of tantamount expense can have uncontrollably fluctuating speculation blunder, and the underlying point can affect the speculation too.

Current introduction methodologies are straightforward and heuristic. Structuring improved instatement systems is a difficult task in light of the fact that the neural system streamlining isn't yet surely known. Most instatement systems depend on accomplishing some pleasant properties when the system is introduced. In any case, we don't have a decent comprehension of which of these properties are saved under which conditions in the wake of learning start to continue. A further difficulty is that some underlying focuses might be beneficial from the perspective of streamlining, however negative from the perspective of speculation. Our comprehension of how the underlying point affects speculation is particularly crude, offering next to zero direction for how to choose the underlying point.

Maybe the main property known with complete assurance is that the underlying parameters need to "break evenness" between different units. In the event that two shrouded units with a similar enactment work are associated with similar sources of info, at that point, these units must have different introductory parameters. On the off chance that they have a similar starting parameter, at that point, a deterministic learning calculation applied to a deterministic cost and display will continually refresh both of these units similarly. Regardless of whether the model or preparing calculation is fit for utilizing stochasticity to figure different refreshes for different units (for instance, on the off chance that one trains with dropout), it is normally best to instate every unit to register a different work from the entirety of different units. This may ensure that no information designs are lost in the invalid space of forwarding proliferation, and no inclination designs are lost in the invalid space of back-engendering. The objective of having every unit process a different work persuades irregular introduction of the parameters. We could unequivocally scan for a huge arrangement of premise works that are all commonly different from one another, yet this regularly brings about an observable computational expense. For instance, on the off chance that we have all things considered the same number of yields as information sources, we could utilize Gram-Schmidt orthogonalization on an underlying weight lattice, and be ensured that every unit figures a very different work from one another unit. Arbitrary introduction from a high-entropy circulation over a high-dimensional space is computationally less expensive and improbable to allot any units to figure a similar capacity as one another.

Regularly, we set the predispositions for every unit to heuristically picked constants, and instate just the loads arbitrarily. Additional parameters, for instance, parameters encoding the contingent fluctuation of an expectation, are normally set to heuristically picked constants, much like the predispositions are.

We quite often introduce every one of the loads in the model to values drawn arbitrarily from a Gaussian or uniform appropriation. The decision of Gaussian or uniform conveyance doesn't appear to make a difference without a doubt; however, it has not been comprehensively examined. The size of the underlying dissemination, be that as it may, has an enormous effect on both the result of the improvement method and on the capacity of the system, to sum up.

Bigger introductory loads will yield a more grounded balance breaking effect, staying away from excess units. They likewise help to abstain from losing signal during advance or back-engendering through the direct part of each layer—bigger qualities in the network bring about bigger yields of framework increase. Beginning loads that are too enormous may, be that as it may, bring about detonating values during forwarding spread or back-engendering. In intermittent systems, huge loads can likewise bring about the disorder (such outrageous affectability to little bothers of the info that the conduct of the deterministic forward engendering strategy seems irregular). Somewhat, the detonating slope issue can be relieved by angle cutting (thresholding the estimations of the inclinations before playing out a slope plunge step). Huge loads may likewise bring about outrageous esteems that reason the actuation capacity to immerse, causing total loss of angle through soaked units. These contending factors decide the perfect beginning size of the loads.

The points of view of regularization and enhancement can give very different experiences into how we ought to instate a system. The enhancement viewpoint proposes that the loads ought to be huge enough to spread data achievement completely; however, some regularization concerns empower, making them littler. The utilization of an improvement calculation, for example, stochastic angle drop that rolls out little steady improvements to the loads and will in general end in regions that are closer to the underlying parameters (regardless of whether due to stalling out in an area of low slope, or due to setting off some early halting measure dependent on overfitting) communicates an earlier that the final parameters ought to be near the underlying parameters. Review from area 7.8 that inclination plummet with early halting is equal to weight rot for certain models. In the general case, slope plummet with early halting isn't equivalent to weight rot; however, it provides a free similarity for pondering the effect of instatement.

Chapter 7

Validating Deep Machine Learning

In view of the likelihood that the classifier reports, you can choose the class (canine or feline) of a photograph dependent on the assessed likelihood determined by the calculation. At the point when the likelihood is higher for a canine, you can limit the danger of making an off-base evaluation by picking the higher possibilities supporting a pooch. The more prominent the likelihood distinction between the probability of a canine against that of a feline, the higher the certainty you can have in your decision. A nearby decision likely happens as a result of some vagueness in the photograph (the photograph isn't clear, or the canine is in reality somewhat cattish). So far as that is concerned, it probably won't be a pooch — and the calculation knows nothing about the raccoon, which is the thing that the image really appears.

Such is the intensity of preparing a classifier: You represent the issue; you offer the models, with everyone deliberately set apart with the mark or class that the calculation ought to learn; your PC prepares the calculation for some time; lastly, you get a subsequent model, which gives you an answer or likelihood. (Naming is a difficult movement in itself, as you find in the parts that pursue.) In the end, a likelihood is only a chance (or a hazard, from another point of view) to propose an answer and find the right solution. Now, you may appear to have tended to each issue and accept that the work is done, yet you should, in any case, approve the outcomes. This part causes you to find why a machine picks up ing isn't only a push-the-button-and-overlook it movement.

Settling up with Sample Errors

At the point when you initially get the information used to prepare the calculation, the information is only an information test. Except if the conditions are very uncommon, the information you get won't be every one of the information that you might get. For example, in the event that you get deals information from your showcasing division, the information you get isn't all the potential deals information on the grounds that except if deals are halted, there will consistently be new information speaking to new deals later on.

In the event that your information isn't every one of the information conceivable, you should consider it an example. An example is a choice, and similarly, as with all determinations, the information could reflect various inspirations about why somebody chose it in such a manner. In this manner, when you get information, the principal question you need to consider is the means by which somebody has chosen it. In the event that somebody chose it arbitrarily, with no particular criteria, you can anticipate that, if things don't transform from the past, future information won't contrast a lot from the information you have close by.

Insights expect that the future won't vary a lot from an earlier time. In this way, you can put together future expectations with respect to past information by utilizing arbitrary testing hypotheses. In the event that you select models haphazardly without a basis, you do have a decent possibility of picking a choice of models that won't vary much from future models, or, in measurable terms, you can expect that the conveyance of your present example will intently look like the dispersion of future examples.

Nonetheless, when the example you get is by one way or another exceptional, it could introduce an issue when preparing the calculation. Truth be told, the unique information could compel your calculation to gain proficiency with an alternate mapping to the reaction than the mapping it may have made by utilizing arbitrary information. For instance, on the off chance that you get deals information from only one shop or just the shops in a solitary district (which is really a particular example), the calculation may not figure out how to estimate the future offers of the considerable number of shops in every one of the locales. The particular example causes issues in light of the fact that different shops might be extraordinary and adhere to various standards from the ones you're watching.

Guaranteeing that your calculation is gaining effectively from information is the explanation you ought to consistently check what the calculation has gained from in-test information (the information utilized for preparing) by testing your theory on some out-of-test information. Out-of-test information is information you didn't have at learning time, and it ought to speak to the sort of information you have to make conjectures.

Searching for Speculation

Speculation is the ability to gain from information close by the general principles that you can apply to every single other datum. Out-of-test information in this way becomes basic to making sense of in the case of gaining from information is conceivable, and to what degree.

Regardless of how huge your in-test dataset is, inclination made by some choice criteria still makes seeing comparable models oftentimes and methodically exceptionally far-fetched in actuality. For instance, in measurements, there is a story about inducing from one-sided tests. It includes the 1936 U.S. presidential political decision between Alfred Landon and Franklin D. Roosevelt in which the Literary Digest utilized one-sided survey data to anticipate the champ.

Around then, the Literary Digest, a good and prominent magazine, surveyed its readers to decide the following leader of the United States, training that it had performed effectively since 1916. The reaction of the survey was strikingly for Landon, with in excess of a 57 percent agreement on the up-and-comer. The magazine likewise utilized such an immense example — in excess of 10 million individuals (with just 2.4 million reacting) — that the outcome appeared to be unassailable: A huge example combined with a huge contrast between the champ and the failure tends not to raise numerous questions. However, the survey was totally fruitless. At last, the room for giving and take was 19 percent, with Landon getting just 38 percent of the vote and Roosevelt getting 62 percent. This edge is the biggest mistake ever for a popular assessment of public sentiment.

What was the deal? Indeed, basically, the magazine addressed individuals whose names were pulled from each phone index in the United States, just as from the magazine's membership list and from programs of clubs and affiliations, assembling in excess of ten million names. Amazing, yet toward the finish of the Great Depression, having a phone, buying in to a magazine, or being a piece of a club implied that you were rich, so the example was made of just princely voters and totally overlooked lower-salary voters, who happen to speak to the larger part (accordingly bringing about a determination inclination). What's more, the survey experienced a nonresponsive predisposition in light of the fact that lone 2.4 million individuals reacted, and individuals who react to surveys will, in general, vary from the individuals who don't. The size of blunder for this specific episode introduced the start of a progressively logical way to deal with testing.

Such old-style instances of choice inclination call attention to that if the choice procedure predispositions an example, the learning procedure will have a similar predisposition. Be that as it may, now and again inclination is unavoidable and hard to spot. For instance, when you go angling with a net, you can see just the fish you get, and that didn't go through the net itself.

Another model originates from World War II. Around then, originators continually improved U.S. warplanes by adding additional protective layer plating to the parts that endured the most shots after coming back from shelling runs. It took the thinking of the mathematician Abraham Wald to bring up that architects really expected to fortify the spots that didn't have slug openings on returning planes.

Starter thinking on your information and testing results with out-of-test models can assist you with spotting or possibly have an instinct of conceivable inspecting issues. Be that as it may, accepting new out-of-test information is regularly troublesome, exorbitant, and requires interest as far as timing. In the business model talked about before, you need to trust that quite a while will test your business determining model — perhaps a whole year — so as to see if your speculation works. What's more, preparing the information for users can spend a lot of time. For instance, when you name photographs of mutts and felines, you have to invest energy marking a bigger number of photographs taken from the web or from a database.

A potential alternative way to using extra exertion is escaping test models from your accessible information test. You save a piece of the information test dependent on a division among preparing and testing information directed by time or by arbitrary examining. On the off chance that time is a significant segment in your concern (for what it's worth in estimating deals), you search for a period mark to use as a separator. Information before a specific date shows up as in-test information; information after that date shows up as out-of-test information. The equivalent happens when you pick information arbitrarily: What you separated as in-test information is only for preparing; what is left is committed to testing purposes and fills in as your out-of-test information.

Becoming Acquainted with the Limits of Bias

Since you find out about the in-test and out-of-test segments of your information, you likewise realize that learning depends a great deal on the in-test information. This segment of your information is significant in light of the fact that you need to find a point of perspective on the world, and likewise, with all perspectives, it tends not to be right, contorted, or just only incomplete. You likewise realize that you need an out-of-test guide to check whether the learning procedure is working. Be that as it may, these viewpoints structure just piece of the image. At the point when you make an AI calculation deal with information so as to figure a specific reaction, you are viably taking a bet, and that bet isn't a result of the example you use for learning. There's additional. For the occasion, envision that you uninhibitedly approach reasonable, fair-minded, in-test information, so information isn't the issue. Rather you have to focus on the technique for learning and anticipating.

In the first place, you should think about what you're wagering that the calculation can sensibly figure the reaction. You can't generally make this supposition since making sense of specific answers is beyond the realm of imagination regardless of what you know ahead of time. For example, you can't completely decide the conduct of people by knowing their past history and conduct. Perhaps an arbitrary impact is associated with the generative procedure of our conduct (the nonsensical piece of us, for example), or possibly the issue boils down to through and through freedom (the issue is additionally a philosophical/strict one, and there are numerous grating suppositions). Therefore, you can figure just a few kinds of reactions, and for some others, for example, when you attempt to foresee individuals' conduct, you need to acknowledge a specific level of vulnerability (which, with karma, is acknowledge capable for your motivations).

Second, you should think about what you're wagering that the connection between the data you have and the reaction you need to foresee can be communicated as a scientific equation or something to that effect and that your AI calculation is really fit for speculating that recipe. The limit of your calculation to figure the scientific recipe behind a reaction is naturally installed in the stray pieces of the calculation. A few calculations can figure nearly everything; others really have a constrained arrangement of choices. The scope of conceivable scientific definitions that a calculation can figure is the arrangement of its conceivable speculation. Thusly, a theory is a solitary calculation determined in the entirety of its parameters and in this way, fit for a solitary, explicit definition.

Arithmetic is awesome. It can depict a great part of this present reality by utilizing some straightforward documentation, and it's the center of AI in light of the fact that any learning calculation has a specific capacity to speak to a numerical definition. A few calculations, for example, direct relapse, unequivocally utilize a particular scientific definition for speaking to how a reaction (for example, the cost of a house) identifies with a lot of prescient data, (for example, advertising data, house area, the surface of the domain, etc.).

A few details are so perplexing and mind-boggling that despite the fact that speaking to them on paper is conceivable, doing so is too troublesome in down to earth terms. Some other complex calculations, for example, choice trees (a theme of the following section), don't have an unequivocal numerical detailing; however, they are versatile to such an extent that they can be set to rough a huge scope of definitions effectively. For instance, think about a basic and effectively clarified detailing.

In a straightforward circumstance of a reaction anticipated by a solitary element, such a model is immaculate when your information orchestrates itself as a line. Notwithstanding, what occurs in the event that it doesn't and rather shapes itself like a bend? To speak to the circumstance, simply watch the accompanying bidimensional portrayals.

At the point when focuses take after a line or a cloud, some mistake happens when you're making sense of what the outcome is a straight line; in this way, the mapping gave by the former definition is some way or another loose. Nonetheless, the mistake doesn't show up efficiently but instead arbitrarily in light of the fact that a few points are over the mapped line and others are underneath it. The circumstance with the bent, formed haze of focuses is extraordinary, on the grounds that this time, the line is at times definite yet on different occasions is efficiently off-base. Here and there focuses are constantly over the line; in some cases, they are underneath it.

Given the straightforwardness of its mapping of the reaction, your calculation will, in general, deliberately overestimate or disparage the genuine guidelines behind the information, speaking to its inclination. The inclination is normal for less complex calculations that can't express complex scientific details.

Remembering Model Complexity

Similarly, as straightforwardness of details is an issue, naturally falling back on map-ping many-sided definitions doesn't generally give an answer. Truth be told, you don't have the foggiest idea about the genuine intricacy of the necessary reaction mapping (for example, regardless of whether it fits in a straight line or in a bent one). In this way, similarly, as straightforwardness may make an inadmissible reaction (allude to Figure 11-1), it's additionally conceivable to speak to the multifaceted nature in information with an excessively unpredictable mapping. In such a case, the issue with a mind-boggling mapping is that it has numerous terms and parameters — and in some outrageous cases, your calculation may have a greater number of parameters than your information has models. Since you should indicate every one of the parameters, the calculation at that point begins retaining everything in the information — the sign as well as the irregular clamor, the mistakes, and all the somewhat explicit qualities of your example.

Now and again, it can even simply remember the models as they seem to be. In any case, except if you're chipping away at issue with a set number of basic highlights with hardly any unmistakable qualities (fundamentally a toy dataset, that is, a dataset with not many models and highlights, hence easy to manage and perfect for models), you're exceptionally improbable to experience a similar model twice, given the huge number of potential mixes of all the accessible highlights in the dataset.

At the point when remembrance occurs, you may have the deception that everything is functioning admirably in light of the fact that your AI calculation appears to have fitted the in-test information so well. Rather, issues can immediately become obvious when you start having it work with out-of-test information, and you see that it produces mistakes in its expectations just as blunders that really change a great deal when you relearn from similar information with a somewhat unique methodology. Overfitting happens when your calculation has gained a lot from your information, up to the point of mapping bend shapes and decides that doesn't exist. Any slight change in the technique or in the preparation information produces whimsical expectations.

Keeping Solutions Balanced

To make extraordinary arrangements, AI models exchange off between straightforwardness (suggesting a higher predisposition) and multifaceted nature (producing a higher difference of evaluations). In the event that you plan to accomplish the best prescient exhibition, you do need to discover an answer in the center by understanding what works better, which you do by utilizing experimentation on your information. Since information is the thing that directs the most suit-capable answer for the forecast issue, you have neither a panacea nor a simple repetitive answer for illuminating all your AI difficulties.

An ordinarily alluded hypothesis in the old numerical stories is the without no lunch hypothesis by David Wolpert and William Macready, which expresses that "any two improvement calculations are comparable when their presentation is found the middle value of over every conceivable issue. On the off chance that the calculations are equal in theory, nobody is better than the different except if demonstrated in a particular, viable issue.

Chapter 8

Preprocess the Machine Data

When fabricating another house, before thinking about any delightful engineering, tasteful expansion, or even furniture intended to improve it, you have to assemble a strong establishment over which to build dividers. What's more, the more troublesome the territory you need to deal with, the additional time and exertion it will take. On the off chance that you disregard to make a durable establishment, nothing based on it can withstand time and nature for long.

A similar issue exists in AI. Regardless of the degree of complexity of the learning calculation, in the event that you don't set up your establishment well — that is, your information — your calculation won't keep going long when tried in genuine information circumstances. You can't get ready information by simply taking a gander at it; you should consume the push to inspect it intently. Shockingly, time spent on cleaning information can take around 80 percent of the all-out time you commit to an AI venture.

Regardless of whether you have enough models close by for preparing both basic and complex learning calculations, they should introduce total esteem in the highlights, with no missing information. Having a fragmented model makes associating every one of the signs inside and between highlights unimaginable. Missing esteems additionally makes it hard for the calculation to get the hang of during preparing. You should take care of the missing information. Frequently, you can overlook missing qualities or fix them by speculating probable substitution esteem. Nonetheless, too many missing esteems render progressively unsure expectations on the grounds that missing data could disguise any conceivable figure; thusly, the all the more missing qualities in the highlights, the more factor and uncertain the forecasts.

Distinguishing Missing Information

As an initial step, tally the number of missing cases in every factor. At the point when a variable has too many missing cases, you may need to drop it from the preparation and test dataset. A decent general guideline is to drop a variable if in excess of 90 percent of its examples are absent.

Some learning calculations don't have the foggiest idea how to manage missing esteems and report blunders in both preparing and test stages, though different models treat them as zero esteems, causing an underestimation of the anticipated worth or likelihood (it's similarly as though some portion of the equation isn't working appropriately). Subsequently, you have to supplant all the missing qualities in your information grid with some appropriate incentive for AI to happen accurately.

Numerous reasons exist for missing information, yet the basic point is whether the information is missing arbitrarily or in a particular request. Irregular missing information is perfect since you can figure it's worth utilizing a basic normal, a middle, or another AI calculation, without such a large number of concerns. A few cases contain a solid inclination toward specific sorts of models. For example, think about the instance of examining the pay of a populace. Well off individuals (for tax assessment reasons, probably) will, in general, conceal their actual salary by answering to you that they don't have the foggiest idea. Destitute individuals, then again, may state that they would prefer not to report their salary inspired by a paranoid fear of negative judgment. In the event that you miss data from specific strata of the populace, fixing the missing information can be troublesome and misdirecting on the grounds that you may imagine that such cases are much the same as the others. Rather, they are very extraordinary.

Along these lines, you can't just utilize normal qualities to supplant the missing qualities — you should utilize complex methodologies and tune them cautiously. In addition, distinguishing cases that aren't missing information at arbitrary is troublesome in light of the fact that it requires a closer review of how missing qualities are related to different factors in the dataset.

At the point when information is absent indiscriminately, you can undoubtedly fix the unfilled qualities since you acquire insights into their actual incentives from different factors. At the point when information isn't absent aimlessly, you can't get great insights from other accessible data except if you comprehend the information related to the missing case. In this manner, in the event that you need to make sense of missing salary in your information, and it is missing in light of the fact that the individual is well off, you can't supplant the missing an incentive with a straightforward normal since you'll supplant it with a medium pay. Rather, you should utilize a normal of the pay of rich individuals as a substitution.

At the point when information isn't absent aimlessly, the way that the worth is missing is enlightening on the grounds that it assists track with bringing down the missing gathering. You can leave the task of searching for the explanation that it's absent to your AI calculation by building another paired component that reports when the estimation of a variable is absent. Thus, the AI calculation will make sense of the best incentive to use as a substitution without anyone else's input.

Picking the Correct Substitution Technique

You have a couple of potential systems to deal with missing information successfully. Your strategy may change in the event that you need to deal with missing qualities in quantitative (values communicated as numbers) or subjective highlights. Subjective highlights, albeit likewise communicated by numbers, are as a general rule alluding to ideas, so their qualities are to some degree discretionary, and you can't seriously take normal or different calculations on them.

When working with subjective highlights, your worth-speculating ought to consistently create whole number numbers, in light of the numbers utilized as codes. Normal methodologies for missing information taking care of are as per the following:

- Replace missing qualities with a processed steady, for example, the mean or the middle worth. In the event that your element is a classification, you should give a particular worth in light of the fact that the numbering is subjective, and utilizing mean or middle doesn't bode well. Utilize this system when the missing qualities are arbitrary.

- Replace missing qualities with an incentive outside the typical worth scope of the component. For example, if the element is sure, supplant missing qualities with negative qualities. This methodology works fine with choice tree-based calculations (for example, those clarified in the past section) and subjective factors.

- Replace missing qualities with 0, which functions admirably with relapse models and institutionalized factors. This methodology is likewise appropriate for subjective factors when they contain paired qualities.

- Interpolate the missing qualities when they are a piece of a progression of qualities attached to time. This methodology works just for quantitative qualities. For example, if your element is day by day deals, you could utilize a moving normal of the most recent seven days or pick the incentive simultaneously the earlier week.

- Impute their worth utilizing the data from other indicator highlights (however never utilize the reaction variable). Especially in R, there are specific libraries like missForest

Another great practice is to make another paired element for every factor whose qualities you fixed. The double factor will follow varieties because of supplanting or ascribing with a positive worth, and your AI calculation can make sense of when it must make extra acclimations to the qualities you really utilized.

In Python, missing qualities are made conceivable, just utilizing the array information structure from the NumPy bundle. Python marks missing qualities with a unique worth that shows up imprinted on the screen as NaN (Not a Number). The DataFrame information structure from the panda's bundle offers techniques for both supplanting missing values and dropping factors.

Making Your Own Features

Once in a while, the crude information you get from different sources won't have the highlights expected to perform AI assignments. At the point when this occurs, you should make your very own highlights so as to acquire the ideal outcome. Making a component doesn't mean making information from meager air, as you find in the areas that pursue. You make new highlights from existing information.

Understanding the Need to make Highlights

One incredible restriction of AI calculations is that it tends to be difficult to figure a recipe that could interface your reaction to the highlights you're utilizing. A few times, this powerlessness to figure happens in light of the fact that you can't delineate reaction utilizing the data you have accessible (implying that you don't have the correct data). In different cases, the data you gave doesn't enable the calculation to adapt appropriately. For example, in case you're displaying the cost of land properties, the outside of the land is very prescient in light of the fact that bigger properties will, in general, cost more. Be that as it may, if rather than the surface, you furnish your AI calculation with the length of the sides of the land (the scope and longitude directions of its corners), your calculation may not make sense of how to manage the data you gave. A few calculations will figure out how to discover the connection between the highlights; however, most calculations won't.

The response to this issue is to highlight creation. Highlight creation is that piece of AI that is viewed as more a workmanship than a science since it infers human mediation in imaginatively blending the current highlights. You play out this undertaking by methods for expansion, subtraction, duplication, and proportion to produce new determined highlights with more prescient power than the firsts.

Realizing the issue well and making sense of how a person would fathom it is a piece of highlight creation. In this way, associating with the past model, the way that land surface interfaces with the property cost are basic information. In the event that surface is absent from your highlights when attempting to figure the estimation of a property, you can recoup such data from the current information — and doing so builds the exhibition of the expectations. Notwithstanding whether you depend on the presence of mind, basic information, or specific ability, you can do a great deal for your machine calculation in the event that you first make sense of what data should work the best for the issue and afterward attempt to have it accessible or get it from among your highlights.

Making Highlights Naturally

You can make some new highlights consequently. One approach to accomplish programmed highlight creation is to utilize polynomial development. Explicit ways are accessible to accomplish polynomial extension, so you make includes consequently in both R and Python. You see some point by point models when working with relapse models and bolster vector machines later in the book. For now, you have to get a handle on the ideas driving polynomial extension.

In polynomial development, you consequently make communications between highlights just as to make powers (for example, registering the square of a component). Collaborations depend on the increase in the highlights. Making another element utilizing increase monitors how highlights will, in general, carry on overall. In this manner, it maps complex connections between your highlights that can allude to uncommon circumstances.

An incredible case of a connection is the commotion produced from a vehicle and the cost of the vehicle. Customers don't acknowledge boisterous autos except if they purchase a games vehicle, in which case the motor commotion is or more that helps the proprietor to remember the vehicle's capacity. It additionally makes onlookers see the cool vehicle, so clamor assumes an incredible job in flaunting on the grounds that commotion will surely stand out for others. Then again, commotion when driving a family vehicle isn't too cool.

In an AI application, in attempting to anticipate the pace of inclination for a specific vehicle, highlights, for example, clamor and the cost of the vehicle are prescient by them-selves. In any case, duplicating the two qualities and adding them to the arrangement of highlights can unequivocally insight into a learning calculation that the objective is a games vehicle (when you increase high clamor levels by a significant expense).

Forces help by making nonlinear relations between the reaction and the highlights, alluding to explicit circumstances. As another model, envision that you need to foresee an individual's yearly costs. Age is a decent indicator on the grounds that as individuals develop old and develop, their life and family circumstances change, as well. Understudies begin poor yet then look for some kind of employment and can assemble a family. From a general perspective, costs will, in general, develop as ages until a specific point. Retirement normally denotes a time when costs will, in general, reduce. Age contains such data; however, it's a component that will, in general, develop, and relating costs to its development doesn't portray the reversal that happens at a particular age. Including the squared component makes a counter impact on age itself, which is little toward the start; however, it develops rapidly with age. The last impact is a parabola, with an underlying development portrayed by a top in costs at a particular age, and afterward a decline.

As referenced at first, knowing ahead of time, such elements (commotion and sports vehicle, utilization, and senior age) can assist you with making the correct highlights. In any case, on the off chance that you don't have a clue about these elements ahead of time, the polynomial extension will naturally make them for you since, given a specific request, it will make collaborations and forces of that request. The request will call attention to the number of augmentations and the greatest capacity to apply to the current highlights. So a polynomial development of request 2 raises every one of the highlights to the subsequent power and duplicates each and every component by all the others. (You get the increase of the considerable number of blends of two highlights.) Clearly, the higher the number, the more new highlights will be made; however, a considerable lot of them will be repetitive and simply add to making your AI calculation overfit the information.

When utilizing polynomial development, you need to focus on the blast of highlights you are making. Forces increment straightly, so on the off chance that you have five highlights and you need the development of request 2, each element is raised by up to the subsequent power. Expanding the request for one just includes another power highlight for every unique component. Rather, cooperations increment dependent on mixes of the highlights up to that request. Actually, with five highlights and a polynomial extension of request 2, every one of the ten one of a kind blends of the coupling of the highlights is made. Expanding the request to 3 will require the production of all the one of a kind blends of two factors, in addition to the one of a kind mixes of three factors, that is, 20 highlights.

Packing Data

Preferably, in AI, you can get the best outcomes when your highlights don't totally associate with one another, and everyone has some prescient power concerning the reaction you're demonstrating. In all actuality, your highlights regularly connect with one another, showing a high level of repetition in the data accessible to the dataset.

Having repetitive information implies that similar data is spread over different highlights. In the event that it's the very same data, it speaks to ideal collinearity. In the event that, rather, it's not the very same data, however, changes here and there, you have collinearity between two factors or multicollinearity between multiple factors.

Repetitive information is an issue that factual hypothesis made answers for address quite a while in the past (on the grounds that measurable calculations can experience the ill effects of multicollinearity). This section introduces the theme from a factual perspective, representing utilizing the ideas of difference, covariance, and connection. You can envision each element as bearing distinctive useful parts, blended in various extents:

- Unique change: The repetition is remarkable to a specific element, and when related or connected with the reaction, it can include an immediate commitment in the expectation of the reaction itself.

- Shared fluctuation: The repetition is basic with different highlights as a result of a causal connection between them. For this situation, if the common data is important to the reaction, the learning calculation will make some troublesome memories picking which highlight to get. What's more, when a component is grabbed for its mutual change, it likewise brings along its particular arbitrary commotion.

- Random commotion segment: Information because of estimation issues or haphazardness that isn't useful in mapping the reaction yet that occasionally, by simple possibility (truly, karma or disaster is a piece of being irregular), can seem identified with the reaction itself.

Chapter 9

Complex Neural Networking

As you venture into the realm of AI, you regularly observe similitudes from the everyday world to clarify the subtleties of calculations. This part shows a group of learning calculations that legitimately determines motivation from how the mind functions.

Beginning with figuring out how a mind forms flag, the connectionists base neural organizes on natural analogies and their segments, utilizing cerebrum terms, for example, neurons and axons as names. In any case, you'll find that neural systems look like simply an advanced sort of direct relapse when you check their math plans. However, these calculations are phenomenally compelling against complex issues, for example, picture and sound acknowledgment, or machine language interpretation. They additionally execute immediately while foreseeing.

Well-conceived neural systems utilize the name profound learning and are behind such control apparatuses as Siri and other computerized colleagues. They are behind the additionally bewildering AI applications also. For example, you see them at work in this mind-blowing exhibition by Microsoft CEO. On the off chance that an AI transformation is going to occur, the expanded learning capacities of neural systems will probably drive it.

Taking In and Imitating from Nature

The center neural system calculation is the neuron (additionally called a unit). Numerous neurons orchestrated in an interconnected structure make up a neural system, with every neuron connecting to the data sources and yields of different neurons. In this way, a neuron can enter highlights from models or the aftereffects of different neurons, contingent upon its area in the neural system.

Something like the neuron, the perceptron, shows up prior in this book, in spite of the fact that it utilizes a less complex structure and capacity. At the point when the analyst Rosenblatt imagined the perceptron, he thought of it as a streamlined scientific adaptation of a mind neuron. A perceptron accepts values as contributions from the close by condition (the dataset), loads them (as synapses do, in light of the quality of the inbound associations), wholes all the weighted qualities, and initiates when the total surpasses a limit. This limit yields an estimation of 1; generally, its expectation is 0. Shockingly, a perceptron can't realize when the classes it attempts to process aren't directly distinguishable. In any case, researchers found that despite the fact that a solitary perceptron couldn't get familiar with the coherent activity XOR (the selective or, which is genuine just when the sources of info are different), two perceptrons cooperating could.

Neurons in a neural system are a further advancement of the perceptron: they take many weighted qualities as information sources, total them, and give the summation as the outcome, similarly as a perceptron does. In any case, they additionally give a progressively modern change of the summation, something that the perceptron can't do. In watching nature, researchers saw that neurons get flag yet don't generally discharge their very own sign. It relies upon the measure of sign got. At the point when a neuron procures enough boosts, it fires an answer; else, it stays quiet. Likewise, algorithmic neurons, in the wake of getting weighted qualities, aggregate them what's more, utilize an actuation capacity to assess the outcome, which changes it in a non-straight way. For example, the enactment capacity can discharge a zero worth except if the info accomplishes a specific limit, or it can hose or improve an incentive by nonlinearly rescaling it, along these lines transmitting a rescaled sign.

A neural system has distinctive actuation capacities, as appeared in Figure 16-2. The straight capacity doesn't have any significant bearing any change, and it's only from time to time utilized on the grounds that it diminishes a neural system to relapse with polynomial changes. Neural organizes usually utilize the sigmoid or the hyperbolic tan.

You get familiar with enactment works later in part; however, note for the time being that actuation capacities unmistakably function admirably in specific scopes of x esteems. Thus, you ought to consistently rescale contributions to a neural system utilizing measurable institutionalization (zero mean and unit fluctuation) or standardize the contribution to the range from 0 to 1 or from − 1 to 1.

Using Feed-Forward to Accelerate

In a neural system, you have first to think about the engineering, which is the manner by which the neural system segments are organized. In opposition to different calculations, which have a fixed pipeline that decides how calculations get and process information, neural systems expect you to choose how data streams by fixing the number of units (the neurons) and their conveyance in layers.

Utilizing a neural system resembles utilizing a stratified separating framework for water: You pour the water from above, and the water is sifted at the base. The water has no real way to return; it just goes ahead and straight down and never along the side. Similarly, neural systems power information highlights to course through the system and blend in with one another just as per the system's design. By utilizing the best design to blend includes, the neural system makes newly formed highlights at each layer and accomplishes better expectations. Tragically, there is no real way to decide the best design without experimentally attempting various arrangements and testing whether yield information predicts your objective qualities subsequent to moving through the system.

The first and last layers assume a significant job. The principal layer, called the information layer, gets the highlights from every datum model handled by the system. The last layer, called the yield layer, discharges the outcomes.

A neural system can process just numeric, consistent data; it can't be compelled to work with subjective factors (for instance, names demonstrating a quality, for example, red, blue, or green in a picture). You can process subjective factors by changing them into a ceaseless numeric worth, for example, a progression of double qualities. At the point when a neural system forms a paired variable, the neuron regards the variable as a nonexclusive number and transforms the double qualities into different qualities, even negative ones, by preparing crosswise over units.

Note the confinement of managing numeric qualities, since you can't anticipate that the last layer should yield a non-numeric mark forecast. When managing a relapse issue, the last layer is a solitary unit. Moreover, when you're working with an order, and you have a yield that must look over a number n of classes, you ought to have n terminal units, everyone speaking to a score connected to the likelihood of the spoke to the class. Subsequently, while ordering a multiclass issue, for example, iris species, the last layer has the same number of units as species. For example, in the old style iris order model, made by the renowned analyst Fisher, you have three classes: setosa, versicolor, and virginica. In a neural system dependent on the Iris dataset, you, in this manner, have three units speaking to one of the three iris species. For every model, the anticipated class is the one that gets the higher score toward the end.

In some neural systems, there are unique last layers, called a softmax, which can change the likelihood of each class depends on the qualities obtained from a past layer.

In order, the last layer may speak to both a segment of probabilities on account of softmax (a multiclass issue in which absolute probabilities total to 100 percent) or an autonomous score expectation (in light of the fact that a model can have more classes, which is a multi-label issue in which added probabilities can be in excess of 100 percent). At the point when the characterization issue is a double grouping, a solitary hub does the trick. Additionally, in relapse, you can have various yield units, everyone speaking to an alternate relapse issue (for example, in estimating, you can have various forecasts for the following day, week, month, etc.).

Neural systems have various layers, every one having its very own dimensions. Since the neural system isolates calculations by layers, realizing the reference layer is significant on the grounds that it implies representing certain units and associations. Subsequently, you can allude to each layer utilizing a particular number and conventionally talk about each layer utilizing the letter l.

Each layer can have an alternate number of units, and the quantity of units situated between two layers directs the number of associations

A framework of loads, for the most part, named with the capitalized Greek letter theta (Θ), speaks to the associations. For simplicity of perusing, the book utilizes the capital letter W, which is a fine decision since it is a network. Consequently, you can utilize W1 to allude to the association loads from layer 1 to layer 2, W2 for the associations from layer 2 to layer 3, etc.

You may see references to the layers between the info and the yield as shrouded layers and tally layers beginning from the principal concealed layer. This is only an alternate show from the one utilized in the book. The models in the book consistently start tallying from the information layer, so the main concealed layer will be layer number 2.

Dimensions speak to the quality of the association between neurons in the network. At the point when the heaviness of the association between two layers is little, it implies that the system dumps esteems streaming among them and sign that taking this course won't probably impact the last expectation. Despite what might be expected, a huge positive or negative worth influences the qualities that the following layer gets along these lines deciding certain forecasts. This methodology is plainly comparable to synapses, which don't remain solitary; however, they are regarding different cells. As somebody develops in understanding, associations between neurons will, in general, debilitate or fortify to dynamic or deactivate certain minds organize cell districts, causing other preparing or a movement (a response to peril, for example, if the handled data flag a perilous circumstance).

Since you realize a few shows with respect to layers, units, and associations, you can begin looking at the activities that neural systems execute in detail. In the first place, you can call information sources and yields in various manners:

- a: The outcome put away in a unit in the neural system subsequent to being prepared by the enactment work (called g). This is the last yield that is sent further along with the system.

- z: The duplication among an and the loads from the W network. Z speaks to the sign experiencing the associations, practically equivalent to water in channels that streams at a sequential weight contingent upon the pipe thickness. Similarly, the qualities got from the past layer get sequential qualities in light of the association loads used to transmit them.

Each progressive layer of units in a neural system dynamically forms the qualities taken from the highlights, the same as in a transport line. As information transmits in the system, it lands into every unit as a worth created by the summation of the qualities present in the past layer and weighted by associations spoke to in the framework W. At the point when the information with included inclination surpasses a specific edge, the enactment work expands the worth put away in the unit; else, it quenches the sign by lessening it. Subsequent to preparing by the enactment work, the outcome is prepared to push forward to the association connected to the following layer. These mean rehash for each layer until the qualities arrive at the end, and you have an outcome.

This shows a detail of the procedure that includes two units pushing their outcomes to another unit. This occasion occurs in all aspects of the system. At the point when you comprehend the section from two neurons to one, you can comprehend the whole feed-forward procedure, in any event, when more layers and neurons are included

Advanced Deep Learning

After backpropagation, the following improvement in neural systems prompted deep learning that is also termed as deep learning. Research proceeded despite AI winter, and neural systems began to exploit the improvements in CPUs and GPUs (the realistic handling units better known for their application in gaming, however, which are in reality incredible registering units for the grid and vector computations). These advancements make preparing neural systems a reachable undertaking in a shorter time and open to more individuals. Research likewise opened a universe of new applications. Neural systems can gain from gigantic measures of information, and in light of the fact that they're more inclined to great change than to predisposition, they can exploit enormous information, making models that persistently perform better, contingent upon the measures of information you feed them. Be that as it may, you need enormous, complex systems for specific applications (to learn complex highlights, for example, the attributes of a progression of pictures) and in this way acquire issues like the evaporating angle.

Truth be told, when preparing an enormous system, the blunder redistributes among the neurons supporting the layers closest to the yield layer. Layers that further away get littler blunders, once in a while excessively little, making preparing moderate if certainly feasible. Because of the investigations of researchers, for example, Geoffrey Hinton, new turnarounds help stay away from the issue of the disappearing slope. The outcome unquestionably helps a bigger system, yet profound learning isn't just about neural systems with more layers and units.

What's more, something innately subjective changed in profound learning as compared to shallow neural systems, moving the worldview in AI from highlight creation (includes that make learning simpler) to include learning (complex highlights consequently made based on the real highlights). Enormous players, for example, Google, Facebook, Microsoft, and IBM, detected the new pattern and since 2012 have begun getting organizations and contracting specialists (Hinton now works with Google; LeCun drives Facebook AI to inquire about) in the new fields of profound learning. The Google Brain venture, run by Andrew Ng and Jeff Dean, set up together 16,000 PCs to compute a profound learning system with in excess of a billion loads, therefore empowering unaided gaining from YouTube recordings.

There is a motivation behind why the nature of profound learning is extraordinary. Obviously, some portion of the thing that matters is the expanded use of GPUs. Together with parallelism (more PCs put in bunches and working in parallel), GPUs enable you to progress completely apply pretraining, new actuation capacities, convolutional systems, and drop-out, an extraordinary sort of regularization not quite the same as L1 and L2. Truth be told, it has been assessed that a GPU can play out specific tasks multiple times quicker than any CPU, permitting a cut in preparing times for neural systems from weeks to days or even hours

Both pertaining and new initiation capacities help tackle the issue of the evaporating angle. New initiation capacities offer better subordinate capacities, and pertaining helps start a neural system with better beginning loads that require only a couple of alterations in the last portions of the system. Progressed pertaining techniques, for example, Restricted Boltzanman Machines, Autoencoders, and Deep Belief Networks expand the information in a solo design by building up starting loads that do not change much during the preparation period of a profound learning system. In addition, they can deliver better highlights speaking to the information and hence accomplish better expectations.

To comprehend the thought behind convolutional neural systems, consider the convolutions channels that, when applied to a framework, change certain pieces of the network, cause different parts to vanish, and make different parts stick out. You can utilize convolution channels for fringes or for explicit shapes. Such channels are additionally useful for discovering subtleties in pictures that figure out what the picture appears. People realize that a vehicle is a vehicle since it has a specific shape and certain highlights, not because they have recently observed each sort of autos conceivable. A standard neural system is attached to its info, and if the information is a pixel framework, it perceives shapes and highlights dependent on their situation on the grid. Convolution neural systems can expand pictures superior to a standard neural system in light of the fact that

- The system practices specific neurons to perceive certain shapes (because of convolutions), with the goal that equivalent ability to perceive a shape doesn't have to show up in various pieces of the system.

- By examining portions of a picture into a solitary worth (an assignment called pooling), you don't have to carefully attach shapes to a specific position (which would make it difficult to turn them). The neural system can perceive the shape in each turn or contortion in this manner, guaranteeing a high limit of speculation of the convolutional arrange.

Finally, drop-out is another sort of regularization that is especially successful with profound convolutional systems, yet it additionally works with all profound learning designs, which acts by incidentally and haphazardly evacuating associations between the neurons. This methodology expels associations that gather just clamor from information during preparing. Likewise, this methodology encourages the system to figure out how to depend on basic data originating from various units, consequently expanding the quality of the right flag went along the layers.

Chapter 10

Decision Tress and Predictors for Learning

In the wake of finding such a large number of unpredictable and incredible calculations, you may be astonished to find that a summation of less complex AI calculations can frequently outflank the most refined arrangements. Such is the intensity of ensembles, gatherings of models made to cooperate to deliver better forecasts. The astounding thing about ensembles is that they are comprised of gatherings of uniquely nonperforming calculations.

Ensembles do not work a lot of uniquely in contrast to the aggregate knowledge of groups, through which a lot of wrong answers, whenever arrived at the midpoint of, gives the correct answer. An English Victorian age analyst defined the possibility of a relationship, portrayed the tale of a group in a region reasonable that could figure the heaviness of a bull accurately after every one of the individuals' past answers were found the middle value of. You can discover comparative models all over the place and effectively reproduce the investigation by soliciting companions to figure the number from desserts in a container and averaging their answers. The more companions who take an interest in the game, the more exact they arrived at the midpoint of the answer.

Karma isn't what's behind the outcome — it's basically the law of huge numbers in real life Even however an individual has a remote possibility of getting the correct answer, the supposition is superior to an arbitrary worth. By collecting surmises, inappropriate answers will, in general, appropriate themselves around the correct one. Inverse wrong answers drop each other when averaging, leaving the critical incentive around which all answers are disseminated, which is the correct answer. You can utilize such a mind-blowing reality from multiple points of view (accord estimates in financial matters and political theories are models) and in AI.

Utilizing Decision Trees

Ensembles depend on an ongoing thought (figured around 1990), yet they influence more seasoned devices, for example, choice trees, which have been a piece of AI since 1950. Choice trees from the start looked very encouraging and speaking to experts because of their usability and comprehension. Overall, a choice tree can without much of a stretch do the accompanying:

- Handle blended sorts of target factors and indicators, with next to no or no component preprocessing (missing qualities are taken care of consequently)

- Ignore excess factors and select just the important highlights

- Work out-of-the case, with no complex hyper-parameters to fix and tune

- Visualize the forecast procedure as a lot of recursive principles masterminded in a tree with branches and leaves, in this way offering the simplicity of translation

Given the scope of positive qualities, you may ask why experts gradually began doubting this calculation following a couple of years. The principal reason is that the subsequent models regularly have high fluctuation in the assessments.

Choice trees parcel the component space into boxes and afterward utilize the containers for grouping or relapse purposes. At the point when the choice limit that isolates classes in a bull's-eye issue is an oval, choice trees can estimate it by utilizing a specific number of boxes.

The visual model appears to bode well and may give you certainty when you see the models set a long way from the choice limit. Be that as it may, in the closeness of the limit, things are very not the same as how they show up. The choice limit of the choice tree is exceptionally uncertain, and its shape is amazingly harsh and squared. The issue is noticeable on bidimensional issues. It unequivocally intensifies as highlight measurements increment and within sight of uproarious (perceptions that are some way or another arbitrarily spread around the component space). You can improve choice trees utilizing some fascinating heuristics that balance out outcomes from trees:

- Keep just the accurately anticipated cases to retrain the calculation

- Build separate trees for misclassified models

- Simplify trees by pruning the less definitive standards

Aside from these heuristics, the best stunt is to fabricate numerous trees utilizing various examples and afterward look at and normal their outcomes. The model in Figure 18-1, demonstrated beforehand, shows that the advantage is quickly obvious. As you construct more trees, the choice limit gets smoother, gradually looking like the hypothetical target shape.

Growing a Backwoods of Trees

Improving a choice tree by repeating it ordinarily and averaging results to get an increasingly broad arrangement seemed like such a smart thought, that it spread, and experts made different arrangements. At the point when the issue is a relapse, the procedure midpoints result from the troupe. Nonetheless, when the trees manage a grouping task, the method can utilize the troupe as a democratic framework, picking the most incessant reaction class as a yield for every one of its replications.

When utilizing a group for relapse, the standard deviation, determined from all the troupe's assessments for a model, can furnish you with a gauge of how sure you can be about the forecast. The standard deviation shows how great a mean is. For grouping issues, the level of trees anticipating a certain class is demonstrative of the degree of trust in the expectation; however, you can't use it as a likelihood gauge since it's the result of a democratic framework.

In bootlashing, you test the models from a set to make another set, enabling the code to test the models on various occasions. In this manner, in a bootstrapped test, you can locate a similar model rehashed from one to commonly.

RF is an arrangement (normally multiclass) and relapse calculation that uses an enormous number of choice tree models based on various arrangements of bootstrapped models and subsampled highlights. Its maker endeavored to make the calculation simple to utilize (small preprocessing and few hyper-parameters to attempt) and reasonable (the choice tree premise) that can democratize the entrance of AI to nonexperts. As it were, in view of its effortlessness and prompt use, RF can enable anybody to apply AI effectively.

What Happens When You Have Random Guesses?

Because of bootstrapping, stowing produces differences decrease by instigating a few varieties is generally comparable indicators. Sacking is best when the models made are not the same as one another and, however, it can work with various types of models; it generally performs with choice trees.

Stowing and its development, the Random Forests, are not the main approaches to use a group. Rather than taking a stab at gathering components' autonomy, an absolute contrarian technique is to make interrelated ensembles of straightforward AI calculations to unravel complex objective capacities. This methodology is called boosting, which works by building models consecutively and preparing each model utilizing data from the past one.

In spite of sacking, which leans towards working with completely developed trees, boosting utilizes one-sided models, which are models that can anticipate basic objective capacities well. Less difficult models incorporate choice trees with a solitary split branch (called stumps), straight models, perceptrons, and Naïve Bayes calculations. These models may not perform well when the objective capacity to figure is mind-boggling (they are powerless students), yet they can be prepared quickly and perform at any rate marginally superior to an irregular fortunate estimate (which implies that they can demonstrate a piece of the objective capacity).

Every calculation in the outfit surmises a part of the capacity well, so when added together, they can figure the whole work. It's a circumstance not very not the same as the account of the visually impaired men and the elephant. In the story, a gathering of visually impaired men needs to find the statue of an elephant, yet each man can feel just a piece of the entire creature. One man contacts the tusk, one the ears, one the proboscides, one the body, and one the tail, which are various parts of the whole elephant.

Just when they put what everyone realized independently together, would they be able to make sense of the elephant's shape. The data for the objective capacity to figure is transmitted from one model to the next by adjusting the first dataset with the goal that the group can focus on the pieces of the dataset that still can't seem to be scholarly.

Deep Learning for Images

AI on pictures works since it can depend on highlights to contrast pictures and partner a picture and another (in light of closeness) or to a particular mark (speculating, for example, the spoke to objects). People can, without much of a stretch, pick a vehicle or a tree when we see one out of an image. Regardless of whether it's the first occasion when that we see a specific sort of tree or vehicle, we can accurately connect it with the correct item (marking) or contrast it and comparable articles in memory (picture review).

On account of a vehicle, having wheels, entryways, a controlling wheel, etc. are on the whole components that assist you with sorting another case of a vehicle among different autos. It hap-pens since you see shapes and components past the picture itself; in this way, regardless of how uncommon a tree or a vehicle might be, on the off chance that it possesses certain attributes, you can make sense of what it is.

A calculation can derive components (shapes, hues, specifics, applicable components, etc.) legitimately from pixels just when you get ready information for it. Aside from

unique sorts of neural systems called convolutional systems, which rank as the cutting edge in picture acknowledgment since they can extricate valuable highlights from crude pictures by themselves, it's constantly important to set up the correct highlights when working with pictures.

Highlight arrangement from pictures resembles playing with a jigsaw — you need to figure out any important specific, surface, or set of corners spoke to inside the picture so as to reproduce an image from its subtleties. This data fills in as the picture highlights and makes up a valuable component for any AI calculation to finish its activity.

Convolutional neural systems channel data over different layers, preparing the parameters of their convolutions (sorts of picture channels); consequently, they can sift through just the highlights significant to the pictures and the errands they're prepared to per-structure. Other uncommon layers, called pooling layers, help the neural net catch these highlights on account of interpretation (they show up in strange parts of the picture) or revolution.

The trained arrange gives you a chance to enter your pictures and acquire an enormous number of qualities that compare to a score on a specific sort of highlight recently learned by the system as a yield. The highlights may compare to a specific shape or surface. What makes a difference to your AI targets is that the most noteworthy highlights for your motivation are among those delivered by the pretrained arrange, so you should pick the correct highlights by making a choice utilizing another neural system, an SVM, or a basic relapse model.

Perceiving Faces Using Eigenfaces

The capacity to perceive a face in the group has become a basic device for some callings. For instance, both the military and law requirements depend on it vigorously. Obviously, facial acknowledgment has utilized for security and different needs also. This model takes a gander at facial acknowledgment in an increasingly broad sense. You may have considered how informal organizations figure out how to label pictures with the proper mark or name. The accompanying model exhibits how to play out this errand by making the correct highlights utilizing eigenfaces.

Eigenfaces are a way to deal with facial acknowledgment dependent on the general appearance of a face, not on its specific subtleties. By methods for the procedure that can block and reshape the fluctuation present in the picture, the reshaped data is dealt with like the DNA of a face along these lines permitting the recuperation of comparative faces (since they have comparable differences) in a large group of facial pictures. It's a less compelling method than removing highlights from the subtleties of a picture, yet it works, and you can execute it rapidly on your PC. This methodology shows how AI can work with crude pixels, yet it's progressively viable when you change picture information into another sort of information.

The model starts by utilizing the Olivetti faces dataset, an open area set of pictures promptly accessible from Scikit-learn. For this investigation, the code isolates the arrangement of named pictures into the preparation and a test set. You have to imagine that you know the marks of the preparation set; however, know nothing from the test set. Therefore, you need to relate pictures from the test set to the most comparable picture from the preparation set.

The Olivetti dataset comprises of 400 photographs taken from 40 individuals (so there are 10 photographs of every individual). Despite the fact that the photographs speak to a similar individual, every photograph has been taken at various occasions during the day, with various light and outward appearances or subtleties (for instance, with glasses and without). The pictures are 64 x 64 pixels, so unfurling every one of the pixels into highlights makes a dataset made of 400 cases and 4,096 factors. It appears to be a high number of highlights, and really, it is. Utilizing Randomized PCA, you can diminish them to a littler and increasingly reasonable number.

The Randomized PCA class is a surmised PCA form, which works better when the dataset is enormous (has numerous columns and factors). The disintegration makes 25 new factors (n_components parameter) and brightening (whiten=True), evacuating some consistent clamor (made by printed and photograph granularity), and superfluous data from pictures in an alternate path from the channels just talked about. The subsequent decay utilizes 25 segments, which is around 80 percent of the data held in 4,096 highlights.

Chapter 11

Improving Deep Learning Models

When your data has been updated, you might be wondering how to improve the data collection and result of the machine learning process. This chapter will help you to explore the strategies that can be applied to increase the productivity of the learning model. With the help of the deep learning tips, you will understand how you can use the test and new data to find the results quicker. These tips will help you to find the best outcomes when you are using the test data. The test data is compiled by keeping the most optimistic result in mind, and when you use the new or raw data for computing, the outcome may vary. Here are some techniques that you can use to improve the outcome achieved by the deep machine learning algorithms.

Studying the Learning Curves

When you are planning to improve the results of the deep learning models, you need to identify the problems in your model. You need to change the training instances to verify the test, and this will help you study the learning curve of the model. With this method, you will be able to identify the issues with the onset and offset data.

You will see many errors when you are working in a biased model and may have many initial differences in the result. This happens due to a lot of variance in the data.

Another thing that you will notice is that the model will behave differently when you increase the test data. The model will face difficulty when it attempts to memorize new and increased data. The model will learn more rules when you change the test data. Studying the learning curve is very important in the deep learning algorithms, as this will help you to know how much data the model can process and how you can increase its efficiency.

When you are getting biased results, you need to reduce the sample size to identify the issue. The model cannot process more data, and this is why the test data needs to be minimized. No matter how much data you place in the system, the bias will not be removed until you find the source of the problem. You need to make the model more complex in order to remove the bias from the data. The interactions between the data can help to reduce bias, and this will help you to study the learning curve in an efficient manner.

The problems related to variance will react well when you add more data. To solve this problem, you need to know where the learning curve converges when you use the onset and offset data. Hyper-parameter tuning and variable selection is used when you are not getting a curve convergence in the model.

Understand the Concept of Cross-Validation

Do you see a large difference between the cross-validation parameter? If yes, then you, the result will be corrupted, and you will need to make changes in the model. The cross-validation can help you to find the problem in an effective manner. You need to know that cross validator is not a good performance predictor and can mislead the new users. Cross-Validation can help you to analyze the deep model and will also provide hints on how to make the model better. The cross-validation will also help you to analyze the out-of-sample errors as well. The CV will correctly find the issues in the test phase and models. The CV differs from the true error results in two basic ways:

Snooping: snooping is the problem in which the information is leaking from the model. This will affect the general result of the model, and when you are studying deep learning, you need to make sure that cross-validation is applied to ensure the best result from the model. The snooping problem occurs when the preprocessing is applied to test data and pooled training. If you use the pooled data for parameter normalization of computing missing data inputs, this will decrease the authenticity of the work.

Incorrect Sampling: The conversion of the classes to the data needs to be done correctly. You should use the right sampling method to pool the data and insert it into the data set.

Finding the Right Error Metric

Attempting to streamline an error metric dependent on the middle error by utilizing a learning calculation won't furnish you with the best outcomes. If you deal with the improvement procedure in a manner that works for your picked metric, then this problem can be drastically reduced. While you are taking care of this issue utilizing information and AI, you have to examine the issue and decide the perfect metric to streamline. Deep learning knowledge and Models can support a great deal and help you increase the proficiency of the model. You can get a significant number of models from scholarly papers and from open AI challenges that cautiously characterize explicit issues regarding information and error/score metric. Search for a challenge whose target and information are like yours, and afterward, check the mentioned metric.

Challenges can give extraordinary motivation to something beyond error metrics. You can without much of a stretch figure out how to oversee information applications, use AI deceives, and perform keen element creation. Check whether the AI calculation that you need to utilize underpins your picked metric. In the event that the calculation utilizes another metric, attempt to guide it via scanning for the best blend of hyper-parameters that can expand your metric. You can accomplish that objective by doing a lattice look for the best cross-validation result utilizing your very own metric as an objective. This will help you to increase the knowledge of the model, and this is very important for scaling in deep learning.

Choosing the Best Hyper-Parameters

Most calculations perform genuinely well out of the container utilizing the default parameter settings. Be that as it may, you can generally accomplish better outcomes by testing diverse hyper-parameters. You should simply do a grid search among potential qualities that your parameters can take and assess the outcomes utilizing the correct error or score metric. The hunt requires some serious energy, yet it can improve your outcomes

At the point when a search takes too long to even think about completing, you can frequently accomplish similar outcomes by dealing with an example of your unique information. Fewer models picked indiscriminately require fewer calculations; however, they, as a rule, allude to a similar arrangement. Another stunt that can spare time and exertion is to do a randomized hunt. In this manner, restricting the quantity of hyper-parameter mixtures to test.

Test Different Models

The no-free-lunch hypothesis ought to consistently be a motivation for you, reminding you not to go gaga for certain learning approaches since they got intriguing outcomes in the past. As a decent practice, test numerous models, beginning with the fundamental ones — the models that have less variance and more bias. You ought to consistently support straightforward arrangements over complex ones. You may find that a straightforward arrangement performs better. For instance, you might need to keep things basic and utilize a straight model rather than a progressively modern, tree-based outfit of models.

Speaking to the presentation of various models utilizing a similar graph is useful before picking the best one to tackle your concern. You can put models used to foresee buyer conduct, for example, a reaction to a business offer, in unique increase outlines, and lift diagrams. These diagrams show how your model performs by partitioning its outcomes into deciles or littler parts. Since you might be intrigued uniquely about the purchasers, who are well on the way to react to your offer, requesting pre-word usages from most to most improbable will underscore how great your models are at anticipating the most encouraging clients.

Testing numerous models and introspecting them (understanding which highlights work better with them) can likewise give recommendations concerning which highlights to trans-structure for include creation, or which highlight to forget about when you make include determinations.

Averaging Models

AI includes building numerous models and making a wide range of forecasts, all with various anticipated error exhibitions. It might amaze you to realize that you can show signs of improvement results by averaging the models together. The guideline is very straightforward: Estimate fluctuation is irregular, so by averaging numerous diverse models, you can upgrade the sign (the right forecast) and decide out the clamor that will frequently drop itself (inverse errors entirety to zero).

Now and then, the outcomes from a calculation that performs well, blended in with the outcomes from a less complex calculation that does not fill in too, can make preferred pre-expressions over utilizing a solitary calculation. Try not to think little of commitments distributed from more straightforward models, for example, direct models, when you normal their outcomes with the yield from progressively advanced calculations, for example, slope boosting.

It is a similar rule you look for while applying gatherings of students, for example, tree packing and boosting outfits. In any case, this time, you utilize the system on complete and heterogeneous models that you plan for assessment. For this situation, if the outcome needs to figure a mind-boggling objective capacity, various models may get various pieces of that capacity. Just by averaging results yield by various basic and complex models, would you be able to surmise a model that you cannot fabricate something else.

Stacking Models

For similar reasons that averaging works, stacking can likewise give you better execution. In stacking, you manufacture your AI models in two (or once in a while much more) stages. At first, this system predicts numerous outcomes utilizing various calculations, with every one of them gaining from the highlights present in your information. During the subsequent stage, rather than giving highlights that another model will learn, you give that model the expectations of the other, recently prepared models.

Utilizing a two-arrange approach is legitimized when speculating complex objective capacities. You can surmise them just by utilizing numerous models together and afterward by consolidating the consequence of the duplication in a keen way. You can utilize a basic strategic relapse or a perplexing tree gathering as a second-organize model.

Applying Feature Engineering

On the off chance that you accept that inclination is as yet influencing your model, you have a minimal decision yet to make new highlights that improve the model's presentation. Each new component can make speculating the objective reaction simpler. For example, if classes are not straightly distinguishable, highlight creation is the best way to change a circumstance that your AI calculation cannot appropriately manage.

Programmed highlight creation is conceivable utilizing polynomial development or the help vector machines class of AI calculations. Bolster vector machines can naturally search for better highlights in higher-dimensional component spaces such that it is both computationally quick and memory ideal.

Notwithstanding, nothing can truly substitute for your aptitude and comprehension of the technique expected to take care of the information issue that the calculation is attempting to learn. You can make highlights dependent on your insight and thoughts on how things work on the planet. People are yet unparalleled in doing as such, and machines can only with significant effort supplant them. Highlight creation is more workmanship than science and without a doubt, human artistry.

Highlight creation is consistently the ideal approach to improve the exhibition of a calculation — when predisposition is the issue, yet additionally, when your model is perplexing and has a high difference.

Selecting Examples and Features

On the off chance that gauge difference is high and your calculation is depending on numerous highlights (tree-based calculations pick highlights they gain from), you have to prune a few highlights for better outcomes. In this unique circumstance, diminishing the number of highlights in your information grid by picking those with the most noteworthy prescient worth is fitting.

When working with direct models, straight help vector machines, or neural networks, regularization is constantly a choice. Both L1 and L2 can decrease the impact of excess factors or even expel them from the model. Dependability choice uses the L1 capacity to reject less helpful factors. The procedure resamples the preparation information to affirm the avoidance.

Searching for More Data

In the wake of attempting all the past recommendations, you may, in any case, have a high fluctuation of forecasts to manage. For this situation, your solitary choice is to expand your preparation set size. Take a stab at expanding your example by giving new information, which could convert into new cases or new highlights.

On the off chance that you need to include more cases, simply hope to see whether you have comparable information close by. You can regularly discover more information; however, it might need naming, that is, and the reaction variable. Investing energy naming new information or approaching other individuals to name it for you may demonstrate extraordinary speculation. Complex models can improve a great deal from extra preparing models in light of the fact that including information makes parameter estimation considerably more dependable and disambiguates cases in which the AI calculation cannot figure out which rule to extricate.

On the off chance that you need to include new highlights, find an open-source information source, if conceivable, to coordinate your information with its entrances. Another incredible method to get both new cases and new includes are by scratching the information from the web. Frequently, information is accessible between various sources or through an application programming interface (API). For example, Google APIs offer numerous land and business data sources. By scripting a scratching session, you can get new information that can put an alternate point of view on your learning issue. New includes help by offering elective approaches to isolate your classes, which you do by making the connection between the reaction and the indicators progressively direct and less uncertain.

Chapter 12

Improving Deep Learning Models 2

When your data has been updated, you might be wondering how to improve the data collection and result of the machine learning process. This chapter will help you to explore the strategies that can be applied to increase the productivity of the learning model. With the help of the deep learning tips, you will understand how you can use the test and new data to find the results quicker. These tips will help you to find the best outcomes when you are using the test data. The test data is compiled by keeping the most optimistic result in mind, and when you use the new or raw data for computing, the outcome may vary. Here are some techniques that you can use to improve the outcome achieved by the deep machine learning algorithms.

Studying the Learning Curves

When you are planning to improve the results of the deep learning models, you need to identify the problems in your model. You need to change the training instances to verify the test, and this will help you study the learning curve of the model. With this method, you will be able to identify the issues with the onset and offset data.

You will see many errors when you are working in a biased model and may have many initial differences in the result. This happens due to a lot of variance in the data.

Another thing that you will notice is that the model will behave differently when you increase the test data. The model will face difficulty when it attempts to memorize new and increased data. The model will learn more rules when you change the test data. Studying the learning curve is very important in the deep learning algorithms, as this will help you to know how much data the model can process and how you can increase its efficiency.

When you are getting biased results, you need to reduce the sample size to identify the issue. The model cannot process more data, and this is why the test data needs to be minimized. No matter how much data you place in the system, the bias will not be removed until you find the source of the problem. You need to make the model more complex in order to remove the bias from the data. The interactions between the data can help to reduce bias, and this will help you to study the learning curve in an efficient manner.

The problems related to variance will react well when you add more data. To solve this problem, you need to know where the learning curve converges when you use the onset and offset data. Hyper-parameter tuning and variable selection is used when you are not getting a curve convergence in the model.

Understand the Concept of Cross-Validation

Do you see a large difference between the cross-validation parameter? If yes, then you, the result will be corrupted, and you will need to make changes in the model. The cross-validation can help you to find the problem in an effective manner. You need to know that cross validator is not a good performance predictor and can mislead the new users. Cross-Validation can help you to analyze the deep model and will also provide hints on how to make the model better. The cross-validation will also help you to analyze the out-of-sample errors as well. The CV will correctly find the issues in the test phase and models. The CV differs from the true error results in two basic ways:

Snooping: snooping is the problem in which the information is leaking from the model. This will affect the general result of the model, and when you are studying deep learning, you need to make sure that cross-validation is applied to ensure the best result from the model. The snooping problem occurs when the preprocessing is applied to test data and pooled training. If you use the pooled data for parameter normalization of computing missing data inputs, this will decrease the authenticity of the work.

Incorrect Sampling: The conversion of the classes to the data needs to be done correctly. You should use the right sampling method to pool the data and insert it into the data set.

Finding the Right Error Metric

Attempting to streamline an error metric dependent on the middle error by utilizing a learning calculation won't furnish you with the best outcomes. If you deal with the improvement procedure in a manner that works for your picked metric, then this problem can be drastically reduced. While you are taking care of this issue utilizing information and AI, you have to examine the issue and decide the perfect metric to streamline. Deep learning knowledge and Models can support a great deal and help you increase the proficiency of the model. You can get a significant number of models from scholarly papers and from open AI challenges that cautiously characterize explicit issues regarding information and error/score metric. Search for a challenge whose target and information are like yours, and afterward, check the mentioned metric.

Challenges can give extraordinary motivation to something beyond error metrics. You can without much of a stretch figure out how to oversee information applications, use AI deceives, and perform keen element creation. Check whether the AI calculation that you need to utilize underpins your picked metric. In the event that the calculation utilizes another metric, attempt to guide it via scanning for the best blend of hyper-parameters that can expand your metric. You can accomplish that objective by doing a lattice look for the best cross-validation result utilizing your very own metric as an objective. This will help you to increase the knowledge of the model, and this is very important for scaling in deep learning.

Choosing the Best Hyper-Parameters

Most calculations perform genuinely well out of the container utilizing the default parameter settings. Be that as it may, you can generally accomplish better outcomes by testing diverse hyper-parameters. You should simply do a grid search among potential qualities that your parameters can take and assess the outcomes utilizing the correct error or score metric. The hunt requires some serious energy, yet it can improve your outcomes

At the point when a search takes too long to even think about completing, you can frequently accomplish similar outcomes by dealing with an example of your unique information. Fewer models picked indiscriminately require fewer calculations; however, they, as a rule, allude to a similar arrangement. Another stunt that can spare time and exertion is to do a randomized hunt. In this manner, restricting the quantity of hyper-parameter mixtures to test.

Test Different Models

The no-free-lunch hypothesis ought to consistently be a motivation for you, reminding you not to go gaga for certain learning approaches since they got intriguing outcomes in the past. As a decent practice, test numerous models, beginning with the fundamental ones — the models that have less variance and more bias. You ought to consistently support straightforward arrangements over complex ones. You may find that a straightforward arrangement performs better. For instance, you might need to keep things basic and utilize a straight model rather than a progressively modern, tree-based outfit of models.

Speaking to the presentation of various models utilizing a similar graph is useful before picking the best one to tackle your concern. You can put models used to foresee buyer conduct, for example, a reaction to a business offer, in unique increase outlines, and lift diagrams. These diagrams show how your model performs by partitioning its outcomes into deciles or littler parts. Since you might be intrigued uniquely about the purchasers, who are well on the way to react to your offer, requesting pre-word usages from most to most improbable will underscore how great your models are at anticipating the most encouraging clients.

Testing numerous models and introspecting them (understanding which highlights work better with them) can likewise give recommendations concerning which highlights to trans-structure for include creation, or which highlight to forget about when you make include determinations.

Averaging Models

AI includes building numerous models and making a wide range of forecasts, all with various anticipated error exhibitions. It might amaze you to realize that you can show signs of improvement results by averaging the models together. The guideline is very straightforward: Estimate fluctuation is irregular, so by averaging numerous diverse models, you can upgrade the sign (the right forecast) and decide out the clamor that will frequently drop itself (inverse errors entirety to zero).

Now and then, the outcomes from a calculation that performs well, blended in with the outcomes from a less complex calculation that does not fill in too, can make preferred pre-expressions over utilizing a solitary calculation. Try not to think little of commitments distributed from more straightforward models, for example, direct models, when you normal their outcomes with the yield from progressively advanced calculations, for example, slope boosting.

It is a similar rule you look for while applying gatherings of students, for example, tree packing and boosting outfits. In any case, this time, you utilize the system on complete and heterogeneous models that you plan for assessment. For this situation, if the outcome needs to figure a mind-boggling objective capacity, various models may get various pieces of that capacity. Just by averaging results yield by various basic and complex models, would you be able to surmise a model that you cannot fabricate something else.

Stacking Models

For similar reasons that averaging works, stacking can likewise give you better execution. In stacking, you manufacture your AI models in two (or once in a while much more) stages. At first, this system predicts numerous outcomes utilizing various calculations, with every one of them gaining from the highlights present in your information. During the subsequent stage, rather than giving highlights that another model will learn, you give that model the expectations of the other, recently prepared models.

Conclusion

Deep machine learning is a concept that has helped scientists and developers to create new machines and applications. The main purpose of this book is to understand the basics of machine learning and how it will affect our lives in the near future. You do not need any basic knowledge regarding machine learning to understand its concept. We have compiled this book in a way that every person who wants to learn machine learning can get good excerpts from the book.

From empirical formulas to concrete information, you will get to know all the important aspects of deep learning, its algorithms, and applications. Deep machine learning is used in various industries, we have highlighted its importance in the future, and you will know about the languages and coding used in this department. You will also get knowledge about machine learning that can be used to perform various tasks in different fields. You need to study the entire book if you are new to machine learning and try to absorb as much reading material as possible.

The Randomized PCA class is a surmised PCA form, which works better when the dataset is enormous (has numerous columns and factors). The disintegration makes 25 new factors (n_components parameter) and brightening (whiten=True), evacuating some consistent clamor (made by printed and photograph granularity), and superfluous data from pictures in an alternate path from the channels just talked about. The subsequent decay utilizes 25 segments, which is around 80 percent of the data held in 4,096 highlights.